Water Governance in Bolivia

This book examines water remunicipalization in Cochabamba since the Water War, offering innovative methodological and theoretical conceptualizations of what it means to be "public," helping to move debates on water services beyond the paralyzing binary of public versus private with a focus on the contested terrain of community engagement around water services.

The Cochabamba Water War of 2000 brought together city residents of all stripes to mobilize against water privatization and gain back public control of the city's water utility. This event catapulted anti-privatization movements around the world, but two decades later, the water movement's vision of democratic water provision remains largely unfulfilled and the city is suffering from a protracted water crisis. Building a typology of participation, this book explores the difficulty in rebuilding a strong public water service in Cochabamba by analyzing the different and often incompatible understandings and interpretations of social control and public participation. Applying this framework to the Bolivian context and, more specifically, to the water and sanitation sector in Cochabamba, the book uncovers whose interests are served and which groups are included or excluded from decision-making and access to water. This exercise illustrates how, in their implementation, participatory practices are not linear and can be distorted or appropriated towards different ends.

This book will be of great interest to students and scholars of water governance, natural resource management, public policy, social movements, and Latin American studies.

Nasya Sara Razavi received her PhD in Human Geography at Queen's University, Canada. Her research lies at the intersection of urban transformations and inequalities in peri-urban Bolivia, as changing infrastructure and severe water shortages shape public participation, gendered insecurities, and everyday practices. She is currently Research Associate at the City Institute at York University, Canada, and lead researcher for the Cochabamba team on the feminist comparative urban research project GenUrb (Urbanization, Gender, and the Global South: A Transformative Knowledge Network).

Routledge Focus on Environment and Sustainability

Monetary Policy and Food Inflation in Emerging and Developing Economies
Abdul-Aziz Iddrisu and Imhotep Paul Alagidede

Mathematical Models and Environmental Change
Case Studies in Long Term Management
Douglas J. Crookes

German Radioactive Waste
Changes in Policy and Law
Robert Rybski

The Sustainable Manifesto
A Commitment to Individual, Economical, and Political Change
Kersten Reich

Phyto and Microbial Remediation of Heavy Metals and Radionuclides in the Environment
An Eco-Friendly Solution for Detoxifying Soils
Rym Salah-Tazdaït and Djaber Tazdaït

Water Governance in Bolivia
Cochabamba since the Water War
Nasya Sara Razavi

For more information about this series, please visit: www.routledge.com/
Routledge-Focus-on-Environment-and-Sustainability/book-series/RFES

Water Governance in Bolivia
Cochabamba since the Water War

Nasya Sara Razavi

Routledge
Taylor & Francis Group

LONDON AND NEW YORK

earthscan
from Routledge

First published 2022
by Routledge
4 Park Square, Milton Park, Abingdon, Oxon OX14 4RN

and by Routledge
605 Third Avenue, New York, NY 10158

Routledge is an imprint of the Taylor & Francis Group, an informa business

British Library Cataloguing-in-Publication Data
A catalogue record for this book is available from the British Library

Library of Congress Cataloging-in-Publication Data
Names: Razavi, Nasya Sara, author.
Title: Water governance in Bolivia: Cochabamba since the water
  war/Nasya Sara Razavi.
Description: Milton Park, Abingdon, Oxon; New York, NY:
  Routledge, 2022. | Includes bibliographical references and index.
Identifiers: LCCN 2021056253 (print) | LCCN 2021056254
  (ebook) | ISBN 9780367770129 (hardback) | ISBN
  9780367770174 (paperback) | ISBN 9781003169383 (ebook)
Subjects: LCSH: Water-supply-Bolivia-Cochabamba. | Water resources
  development-Economic aspects-Bolivia-Cochabamba. | Water rights-
  Bolivia-Cochabamba. | Water security-Bolivia-Cochabamba.
Classification: LCC HD1696.B54 C6358 2022 (print) | LCC
  HD1696.B54 (ebook) | DDC 333.9100984/23-dc23/
  eng/20211206
LC record available at https://lccn.loc.gov/2021056253
LC ebook record available at https://lccn.loc.gov/2021056254

ISBN: 978-0-367-77012-9 (hbk)
ISBN: 978-0-367-77017-4 (pbk)
ISBN: 978-1-003-16938-3 (ebk)

DOI: 10.4324/9781003169383

Typeset in Times New Roman
by Apex CoVantage, LLC

For FERN

Pujio yacuta
apay chajrayquiman.
Lark'ata ruay cunan tuta,
k'aya paqarin
chu'ya yacu chamunanpaj
saphi sara uijiananpaj.

Fernando Villena Villegas

Contents

Tables and Figures

Tables

Figures

Acknowledgements

I am grateful to everyone in Bolivia who made this book possible in a big or small way. I am indebted to all who welcomed me into their offices, communities, and often their homes, to share with me their time, knowledge, and experiences that inform this work and my learning.

This research was possible thanks to the International Development Research Centre Doctoral Award (107473–99906075–018) and the Queen's University Dean Travel Award. This research was carried out following clearance by Queen's University's General Research Ethics Board (GREB) process (GGEO-160–13 #6011157). Portions of this work appear in the publication Razavi, N.S. (2019). Social control and the politics of public participation in water remunicipalization, Cochabamba, Bolivia. *Water*, *11*, 1455. Thank you to Hannah Ferguson, John Baddeley, and the editorial and production team at Routledge.

Thank you to Carlos Crespo for the regular discussions, sharing his deep knowledge of Bolivian politics, and for giving me a desk at CESU-UMSS. I am thankful to Rocio Bustamante for her generosity with her time and expertise, and for always including me in Centro AGUA activities. Thanks to Fernando Antezana, Oscar Campanini, Sonia Dávila-Poblete, Manuel de la Fuente, Alfredo Duran, Pablo Regalsky, CEDIB, CENDA, and special thanks to Carmen Ledo for her encouragement and enthusiasm for the project. Thank you to Ida Peñaranda for her friendship and accompanying me on field visits. Thank you to Marcela Olivera and Red VIDA for facilitating connections. Thanks to Maria Eugenia Flores Castro, Oscar Olivera, Anacleto Chaquicallata, Abraham Grandydier, RoseMary Irusta, Giovanna Caneda, Stefano Archidiaco, Francesca Minelli, Ramiro Flores, Gustavo Heredia, Humberto Gandarillas, Abel Lizarazu, Orlando Luisaga, Jhonny Maita Vargas, Ruben Mendez, Renato Montayo, Julia Montes, Monika Okabe, Edgar Paniagua, Gregory Paz, Juan Cabrera, Fernando Perez, Ramiro Rios, Hernán Orellana, Michael Roca, Julio Rodriguez, Juan Aguilar, Jorge Alvarado, Leonardo Anaya, José Antonio Aranibar Zarte, Jimena Ayarao,

Alejandra Campos, Soledad Delgadillo, Omar Fernández, Raúl Flores Mejia, Rocio Fuentes, Luis Salazar, Ronald Salazar, Betty Soto, Edgar Varnoux, José Villaba, Gaston Zeballos, and special thanks to Samuel Gareca. My sincerest appreciation to all of the research interlocutors I cannot name here. Thanks to Susan Spronk for the introduction to Bolivia and fieldwork all those years ago. Thank you to Lee Cridland and the Bolivia Cultura staff. Gracias a mi segunda familia, Denisse, Marco, Luis, y la mamà for opening their home and hearts to me once more. *La ciudad de eterna primavera alivió los momentos difíciles del trabajo de campo, con gente y momentos que nunca olvidaré, gracias eternamente.*

This book would not have been possible without the support, time, and effort of many mentors. I owe a debt of gratitude to David McDonald, a compassionate and brilliant scholar to emulate. Thank you for your (extremely prompt) feedback, guidance, patience, and for the confidence you instilled in me. I am thankful to Beverley Mullings and Laura Cameron, for your endless support and enthusiasm, and to Cathie Krull, and Catherine Conaghan, thank you for your insights and comments on this work. Thank you to Warren Mabee, Neal Scott, Anne Godlewska, and everyone who helped me and showed me kindness at the Department of Geography and Planning at Queen's University.

To my friends and the SSBs for keeping me laughing, and to my friends and colleagues at Queen's, thank you for the camaraderie and sympathy. Special thanks to the stellar Ashley Rudy for her support and generously creating maps for this book. To my sister Rox, who inspires me everyday, and Leo (and Gia!), thank you for your advice and for always being in my corner despite the distance. Thanks to Guillaume, for the constant encouragement, understanding, and care over the years, je t'aime. Finally, I thank my parents, Éléonore and Feri, for being my loudest cheerleaders, for always supporting me in every possible way, and for their love.

Glossary of terms and abbreviations

AAPS	Fiscal and Social Control Authority (*Autoridad de Fiscalización y Control Social*)
Aguatero	Water vendor
APAAS	Association of Production and Administration of Water and Sanitation (*Asociación de Producción y Administración de Agua y Saneamiento*)
ASICA-SUDD-EPSAS	Departmental Association of Community Water Systems of the South and Provider Entities of Water and Sanitation Services (*Asociación de Sistemas Comunitarios de Agua del Sud, Departamental y Entidades Prestadoras de Servicio de Agua y Saneamiento*)
Campesino	*Campesino* is a term denoting people residing in the countryside who may identify as Indigenous culturally or linguistically
La Coordinadora	Coalition for the Defence of Water and Life (*Coordinadora por la Defensa del Agua y la Vida*)
COB	Bolivian Workers' Central (*Central Obrera Boliviana*)
CSUTCB	Bolivian Unitary Syndical Peasant Workers Confederation (*Confederación Sindical Única de Trabajadores Campesinos de Bolivia*)
DESCOM	Community Development and Institutional Capacity Building (*Desarrollo Comunitario y Fortalecimiento Institucional*)
DGA	Cochabamba Department Water Directorate (*Dirección de Gestión del Agua del Gobierno Autónomo de Cochabamba*)

ELFEC	Cochabamba electric utility company (*Empresa de Luz y Fuerza Électrica Cochabamba*)
EMAGUA	Project-Executing Agency of Environment and Water (*Empresa Ejecutora de Medio Ambiente y Agua*)
ENDE	National Electricity Company (*Empresa Nacional de Electricidad Bolivia*)
EPSA	Potable Water and Sewerage Service Provider (*Entidad Prestador de Saneamiento y Agua*)
FEDECOR	Cochabamba Department Federation of Irrigators' Organization (*Federación Departamental Cochabamba de Organizaciones de Regantes*)
Junta vecinal	Neighbourhood committee or association
LPP	Law of Popular Participation (*Ley de Participación Popular*)
MAS	Movement Towards Socialism (*Movimiento Al Socialismo*)
MMAyA	Ministry of Environment and Water (*Ministerio del Medio Ambiente y Agua*)
PMM	Metropolitan Master Plan for water services in Cochabamba (*Plan Maestro Metropolitano de Agua y Saneamiento del Area Metropolitano de Cochabamba*)
OTB	Grassroots Territorial Organization (*Organizaciones Territoriales de Base*) established through the LPP
SEMAPA	Cochabamba's Municipal Water and Sewerage Services (*Servicio Municipal de Agua Potable y Alcantarillado Cochabamba*)
SENASBA	National Service for the Sustainability of Sanitation Services (*Servicio Nacional para la Sostenibilidad de Servicios en Saneamiento Básico*)
Usos y costumbres	Form of collective management based on social agreements negotiated and renegotiated over time

1 Introduction

Remunicipalization

Putting the focus on public

Reclaiming public water utilities has been successful in several municipalities around the world, demonstrating the viability of public alternatives for water service delivery (Balanyá et al., 2005; Kishimoto & Petitjean, 2017; Pigeon et al., 2012). Research shows over 1,400 cases of successful remunicipalization, returning to public services, in more than 2,400 cities globally (Kishimoto et al., 2020). The Water War in Cochabamba, Bolivia, is a celebrated example of citizens mobilizing against the privatization of the municipal water company to oust the private foreign enterprise from the country. The mobilizations for the democratization of water in 2000 and beyond have demonstrated that privatization is neither a desired nor a viable option in Cochabamba. However, the public water system remains a work in progress as the people of Cochabamba continue to struggle for better public services today. As a starting point for analysis, I examine the concept of "social control," a demand made by the water movement in Bolivia for collaborative participatory governance and greater influence in decision-making that has been incorporated to varying degrees in Bolivia's overarching water policies.

Academic literature has primarily focused on anti-privatization resistance rather than post-privatization recovery. Progressive research is, however, now moving away from the anti-privatization debate and towards building a greater conceptual and empirical understanding of public alternatives. This book contributes to this literature through the analysis of water remunicipalization in Cochabamba to help provide insights into what has worked with the new public entity, what has not, and where the public water system could be strengthened, being mindful of how power dynamics are reproduced or addressed in alternative models of governance. Remunicipalization is the most widely used term referring to "the return of water services to public ownership and management following the termination of private contracts"

DOI: 10.4324/9781003169383-1

(Lobina, 2017, p. 149). It typically, though not exclusively, entails a return to operation at the municipal level (McDonald & Ruiters, 2012). Building on a growing literature and experiences with the remunicipalization of public water services around the world, my research aims to contribute to the methodological evaluation and theoretical conceptualization of public alternatives.

Although most countries began their water services via private investments, it became clear by the early 20th century that private companies were largely unable or uninterested in investing in water infrastructure owing to the low profitability of such investments. As water and sewage systems are natural monopolies, it was also viewed as more efficient to provide water through a centralized administration rather than through competing firms using parallel infrastructure systems. As was the case with health care, water provision came to be considered a state responsibility due to the universal social and economic benefits for citizens, not to mention water's importance to industrial development and the economic health of the developmental state. Therefore, after World War II, access to water, basic services, and sanitation came under public sector management around the world, although the endeavour was typically more successful in the Global North than in the Global South due to resource availability and political commitment (Bakker, 2003b; Bennett, 1995).

The story has been very different since the 1970s. Accompanying the neoliberal policy shift of the past few decades has been an objection to the concept that states should hold the primary responsibility for providing access to water. Proponents of privatization have cited "state failure" in providing universal water access in policy documents and reports (Bakker, 2013; Howell & Pearce, 2001). The 1992 Dublin Principles defined water as an "economic good," and presented the argument that past failures to attribute an economic value to water had led to wasteful use and scarcity of water resources in developing countries (Bakker, 2007; Budds & McGranahan, 2003; Castro, 2009). Thus, privatization[1] of the water sector was presented as the best solution to poor public sector performance.

Under pressure from the World Bank and the International Monetary Fund, many governments of developing countries in Latin America, Africa, and Asia were pressured to sell off their public water systems.[2] These policies have served to normalize the occurrence of transnational corporations providing public services. However, it is important to note that the lines between public and private are not as distinct as they are often depicted. The majority of the largest donor-funded water projects consist of public–private partnerships (PPPs) as collaborations between private companies and states (Boag & McDonald, 2010).

Substantial literature critical of water privatization emerged as a result of the impacts of the increased commercialization of water systems (Barlow, 2007; Budds & McGranahan, 2003; Hall & Lobina, 2007; Swyngedouw, 2005). The imposition of water privatization by international organizations has raised questions about democratic control and the limitations placed on the decision-making capacity of local government and people. However, while the interests of multinational corporations are clearly promoted, local elites often support and benefit from privatization as well (Acemoglu & Robinson, 2012; Bakker, 2003a; Conaghan & Malloy, 1994; Estrin & Pelletier, 2018; Kohl, 2002; Yeboah, 2006). Privatization has mostly failed in its desired objectives and has not proven to be more efficient or effective than the public sphere in water provision. While privatization was purported to solve the problem of uneven access—a panacea to water problems—it has not led to full expansion of service delivery, and the costs of limited expansion typically fall on consumers and taxpayers (Budds & McGranahan, 2003; Hall & Lobina, 2007). In Cochabamba, user fees skyrocketed to unaffordable levels, cutting off the poorest households from accessing water. Similar experiences with water privatization occurred in Argentina, South Africa, Chile, and Uruguay (Bakker, 2000). Importantly, in the case of Cochabamba, the private contract granted the concession access to sources of water traditionally used collectively by rural farmers. This provoked a movement to reaffirm the importance of regaining social control of the water systems.

Much of the academic literature on the Water War in Bolivia focuses on its success as an anti-privatization victory, but the ongoing struggle for better public services in Cochabamba has not been adequately documented or assessed. This is reflective of the tendency in the debates on commodification to reject privatization in favour of public alternatives yet stop short of exploring a deeper conceptualization of what an alternative means and how it might unfold on the ground. Researchers often talk about the need for alternatives to water privatization, yet their focus is on highlighting the destructive processes of privatization and social movement strategies to overcome them rather than on explicit investigations of what else might be done.

Following the failure of many private sector water contracts, discussions of alternative water supply models have increasingly invoked "public" or "community." However, without defining the concepts, these models can actually serve to extend the logic of commercialization, as can be observed in the surge of public–private–community partnerships (PPCPs), water provision resulting from partnerships typically between communities and small-scale private businesses (Franceys & Weitz, 2003). There is, however, also a push to remove profit-driven private sector involvement in water delivery.

Social movements around the world view water as essential for human survival and defend water as part the global commons, seeking progressive ways to manage water services via state and non-state mechanisms.

A new research agenda is underway as authors call for a deeper analysis of public alternatives and their consequences (Balanyá et al., 2005; Driessen, 2008; Kishimoto & Petitjean, 2017; Kishimoto et al., 2020; Lobina, 2017; McDonald, 2018, 2019; McDonald & Ruiters, 2012; McDonald et al., 2020; Pigeon et al., 2012; Sick, 2008; Spronk, 2010). The literature on public alternatives does not constitute a consistent theoretical approach, but has made advances in the conceptualization of public and how we understand its possibilities and limitations. So, too, is there a growing comparative literature exploring different experiences of public alternatives, using methodologies grounded in a normative framework to assess their success (McDonald, 2016; McDonald & Ruiters, 2012). The following criteria have been employed to refer to broad categories of evaluation, all of which contain a range of finer-tuned sub-categories with reference to criteria such as gender and spatiality: participation, equity, accountability, transparency, quality, transferability, efficiency, sustainability, solidarity, public ethos. These terms establish universal criteria for public services, yet are flexible enough to be culturally specific and appropriate, allowing for contextualized accounts of water access and distribution while still enabling the comparison of cases in other parts of the world.

This book builds upon this emerging literature on public alternatives as a starting point to understanding efforts to rebuild public water services in Cochabamba, with a particular focus on the criteria of participation. The slogans of the Cochabamba water movement suggest that water should not simply be a means for economic profit or state control but a public good that is essential for life and accessible to all citizens, driven by community engagement. Demands for social control revolve around local stewardship, with communities being part of the new public solution. Applying the concept of social control allows us to better see the obstacles to and opportunities for creating a public water alternative and can provide insights into the processes through which political power is exerted by varying actors in the development of water systems (Swyngedouw, 1997).

Guiding questions and fieldwork

Grassroots resistance to the commercialization of water in Cochabamba has produced a narrative of public control of water services that envisions water as a public good. The water movement in Cochabamba shifted from an anti-privatization battle to a struggle to build an alternative system. This book examines why, almost two decades after the Water War, the democratic vision of Cochabamba's water movement is still unfulfilled and why water access remains extremely fragmented. It seeks to uncover the obstacles in realizing a progressive public vision of water delivery but also sheds light on opportunities to strengthen the public utility. In doing so, this project focuses on the movement's demand for social control, a collective form of water management with greater citizen participation. I examine the various meanings of social control and how different understandings of it have been incorporated into the new public model (or not) for water services in Cochabamba. In particular, I want to see how participatory mechanisms have developed and whether they meet demands for social control made by citizens. As such, the research is guided by the following questions: 1) How is social control defined by actors in Cochabamba, and how has it changed over time? 2) How have calls for social control been integrated into managerial, operational, and technical responsibilities of water service provision in the city? and 3) How does social control facilitate inclusion or exclusion amongst water users in Cochabamba, and does it reproduce or confront inequities?

My research methodology was geared towards gathering information on the depth and scope of participation, how participation is formalized or institutionalized, and if the forms of participation can be sustained in the long term. The research comprises a study of Cochabamba to give a contextual account of water access and distribution. The use of a case study follows Snow and Trom's (2002, p. 147) definition that includes the following: 1) investigation and analysis of an instance or variant of some bounded social phenomenon that 2) seeks to generate a richly detailed and "thick" elaboration of the phenomenon studied through 3) the use and triangulation of multiple methods or procedures that include but are not limited to qualitative techniques.

The methods I used to undertake this research included text analysis, participant observation, and in-depth interviewing, incorporating Smith's (2007, p. 413) feminist institutional ethnography approach, which is a method of inquiry that

> explores and explicates social relations and powers from the standpoint of people in their everyday worlds . . . [to learn] from the actualities of what people are doing and from what they have to tell her or him about their everyday lives.

Using this approach puts an emphasis on social relations, "the sequences of action in which people are involved at different stages but not necessarily directly engaged in a shared work process," thereby starting with the actions and everyday experiences of people participating in the management of

Cochabamba's water services and then exploring how people's activities and contributions are coordinated through these activities (Smith, 2007). This approach also emphasizes institutions' use of texts to coordinate people's work, how they reflect social relations, and how they are actioned. I pay attention to how the concept of social control is included in the laws, policies, and procedures that are key to water governance in Cochabamba and the kinds of outcomes this entails for water users.

During my fieldwork, I explored how the people of Cochabamba envision public water services and how the articulations of the demand for social control have shifted over time. I delved into the specific demands people made and how they were framed, acknowledging distinctions made by different actors in an effort to highlight the perspectives of well-organized but marginalized populations. I focused on how social control in water services satisfies users' needs and demands in areas where people want to see change. I also investigated the strategies used by organizations and community groups to strengthen water services.

This analysis aimed to identify the different needs and relationships between actors and where network building between institutions can address possible inequities. Gaining an understanding of the positions of different groups, their views of public water systems, and the socio-economic and political relationships between these groups helps identify points of contention as well as common ground for strengthening the water services. Examining the roles that various actors play in participatory governance and their perceptions of reforms since 2000 is key to understanding Cochabamba's current water governance dynamics and to uncovering the gap between the demands for a strong public water utility on the one hand and the lack of adequate services and uneven water access on the other.

To frame the study of Cochabamba city, I also examine water governance structures in Bolivia more generally and trace how these have changed since the shift towards socialism in Bolivia in 2005, focusing on the degree of incorporation of social control into policy and procedures. Examining these changes is fundamental to understanding governance in a context of competing water demands and the tensions that can arise between Bolivian state law and customary law. At the local scale, I gathered technical and institutional information on Cochabamba's official municipal water company, Semapa, and the small-scale service providers that supply water to communities outside of Semapa's networks. I examine how the different models of water provision overlap and differ and how they interact to assess the unique challenges faced in providing reliable services to a diverse public, with a focus on the low-income periphery of Cochabamba.

I made three fieldwork trips to Bolivia to collect primary data on Cochabamba's water services sector (October to December 2013; January to December 2014; June to August 2016). During these trips I was affiliated with Red VIDA (*Vigilancia Interamericana para la Defensa y Derecho al Agua*—Inter-American Network for the Defence of the Right to Water), a network of organizations that work collaboratively to defend the right to water in the Americas that have headquarters in Cochabamba. Through the affiliation with Red VIDA, I was in contact with networks of organizations that work directly with communities in the more marginalized Southern Zone, notably ASICA-SUDD-EPSAS (Departmental Association of Community Water Systems of the South and Provider Entities of Water and Sanitation Services—*Asociación de Sistemas Comunitarios de Agua del Sud, Departamental y Entidades Prestadoras de Servicio de Agua y Saneamiento*). Given time and resource constraints it was not possible to interview a statistically representative sample of Cochabamba residents. However, through my contacts at Red VIDA, it was possible to collect various grassroots opinions from different geographic and socio-economic sectors of the city, focusing on senior leaders of community-based water organizations that operate in the Southern Zone of Cochabamba. I was able to reach out to local water committees and cooperatives to learn about the challenges faced by community members of different districts. I engaged in participant observation, that is "observing people in their own milieux and participating in their activities" (Devine, 1995, p. 137) by attending district water meetings and the meetings held by Semapa as part of the social control procedures. I also assisted on research outings and workshops with Orellana Consulting Group and Centro AGUA (Andean Centre for Water Use and Management–*Centro Andino para la Gestión y Uso de Agua*) to understand water challenges and observe how ideas are discussed and exchanged and the power dynamics in community decision-making. In 2016, I was able to spend two months with the Maria Auxiliadora women's initiative to observe their unique form of social control and particular struggles for access to water provision. That same year I attended the water summits that were organized and held in response to the ongoing water crisis.

While in the field, I collected secondary data such as institutional reports, journals, books, and newspapers that are only available in Bolivia (in Spanish) at the libraries of the Bolivian Centre for Documentation and Information (CEDIB), the Centre for Andean Communication and Development (CENDA), and the resource collection at Red VIDA; all three institutions are located in Cochabamba. I reviewed these sources in an effort to contextualize public water alternatives in Cochabamba within the "local cultural and political spaces, [and] global flows of policies, capital, personnel, and discourse" (Paulson & Gezon, 2005, p. 14). This data informed the analysis on the shifts in water and sanitation policy in the context of post-privatization in Cochabamba and, more broadly, the turn to socialism in the country.

Another group of interviews was conducted with people who hold key positions in utility management, water regulation, policy making, small domestic water operations, unions, and non-governmental organizations (NGOs). Once again, the sampling here was broadly representative of the most important and influential actors in the water sector in Cochabamba. I conducted interviews with representatives of the official municipal utility service provider Semapa, including the General Manager, Head of Planning, Head of Operations, Head of Transparency, worker's union representatives, representatives on the Board of Directors, and former Semapa citizen representatives. Key insights were gathered from regional experts and intellectuals and actors that played crucial roles during and after the Cochabamba Water War, such as Marcela Olivera, activist and Program Lead at Red VIDA and the Latin American Branch of Food and Water Watch, and Oscar Olivera, union activist and a founding member of *La Coordinadora*. I interviewed program coordinators in key NGOs that played a major role in recent water reforms, as well as management, water and sanitation experts, and engineers from various international development agencies, including the German development agency GIZ (*Deutsche Gesellschaft für Internationale Zusammenarbeit*) and Italian development institution CeVI (*Centro di Volontariato Internazionale*), instrumental in funding and developing water projects in the region. Finally, I conducted interviews with government officials and civil servants responsible for water and sanitation at the local level in the mayor's office as well as at the departmental and national levels within the Water Ministry.

In total, I conducted 75 interviews with a cross-section of people in government, academia, civil society, and community leaders. I make use of direct quotes in the book; in certain places I found it more useful contextually to identify speakers by their profession or position rather than by name. The formal interviews were supplemented by informal conversations with scholars, water experts, and end users during my fieldwork. These informal conversations and the interviews provided insights from the most senior and influential people related to the post-privatization water service debates in Cochabamba as well as end user experiences. Key themes that emerged from the interviews and conversations around class dynamics and differentiated access to water inform the analysis throughout the book.

Book structure

This book tells the story of the complicated process of remunicipalization in Cochabamba and the struggle to rebuild successful public water services for the population. Chapter 2 serves as an introduction to Cochabamba, briefly recounting the Water War of 2000 and the political context which led to these pivotal days of mobilization before providing an overview of the fragmented water access and distribution in and around the city. Using the concept of the hydrosocial cycle, this chapter traces each point of the Cochabamba waterscape to capture the differentiated access and power dynamics embedded in everyday water practices and water governance structures (Castree, 2008; Swyngedouw, 2007).

In Chapter 3 I develop the conceptual framework from which I analyze public participation and social control in Bolivia. Here, I identify the different understandings and interpretations of participation based on intent, which can be categorized into three overarching types of participation. The first, transformative participation, uses public participation as a tool to create a radical shift in the existing structures of inequality in order to redistribute power. The second, reformative participation, is intended to modify decision-making processes without disturbing the wider power structures; in fact, the intent is often to strengthen market systems. These categories also bring to light a third, token form of participation, which I call nominal participation. In all three cases, I identify the main elements of how they operate, including intended outcomes, main actors, and the tools and practices used to implement each kind of participation. In the second half of the chapter, I apply this typology to Bolivia in general to examine the often contradictory local forms and spaces of participation and both the tensions and opportunities they encompass.

Chapter 4 applies this participation framework to the Bolivian water sector and specifically to the city of Cochabamba. The framework serves to untangle competing perspectives of participation and social control and uncover whose interests are served and which groups are included or excluded from access to water and decision-making. This analysis reveals how transformative participation has failed to take hold within the municipal water service provider in Cochabamba and sheds light on the implications for building a universal public water system in a city that maintains parallel but uneven water networks. In Chapter 5, I shift my focus to broader water governance initiatives—namely the Misicuni Multipurpose Project, the Metropolitan Master Plan, and the Water Agenda—that offer competing visions of how to address the water crisis in Cochabamba. Finally, Chapter 6 provides a summary of the main research findings and offers concluding reflections on potential reforms for establishing more equitable water services in Bolivia.

Notes

1 Here "privatization" follows Budds and McGranahan's (2003) definition of "processes that increase the participation of formal private enterprises in water and

sanitation provision, but do not necessarily involve the transfer of assets to the private sector." In Latin America, French style concession contracts (spanning terms of 25 to 40 years) have been the most common type of privatization.
2 From 1987–2000, 183 water and sewerage projects were established (in non-OECD countries) with participation of the private sector (Bakker, 2003b).

References

Acemoglu, D., & Robinson, J. (2012). *Why nations fail: The origins of power, prosperity and poverty*. Crown.

Bakker, K. J. (2000). Privatizing water, producing scarcity: The Yorkshire Drought of 1995. *Economic Geography*, *76*(1).

Bakker, K. J. (2003a). Archipelagos and networks: Urbanization and water privatization in the South. *The Geographical Journal*, *169*(4), 328–341. https://doi.org/10.1111/j.0016-7398.2003.00097.x

Bakker, K. J. (2003b). From public to private to . . . mutual? Restructuring water supply governance in England and Wales. *Geoforum*, *34*(3), 359–374. https://doi.org/10.1016/S0016-7185(02)00092-1

Bakker, K. J. (2007). The "commons" versus the "commodity": Alter-globalization, anti-privatization and the human right to water in the Global South. *Antipode*, *39*(3), 430–455. https://doi.org/10.1111/j.1467-8330.2007.00534.x

Bakker, K. J. (2013). Neoliberal versus postneoliberal water: Geographies of privatization and resistance. *Annals of the Association of American Geographers*, *103*(2), 253–260.

Balanyá, B., Brennan, B., Hoedeman, O., Kishimoto, S., Lobina, E., & Terhorst, P. (2005). *Reclaiming public water: Achievements struggles and visions from around the world*. Transnational Institute.

Barlow, M. (2007). *Blue covenant: The global water crisis and the coming battle for the right to water*. New Press.

Bennett, V. (1995). *The politics of water: Urban protest, gender, and power in Monterrey, Mexico*. University of Pittsburgh Press.

Boag, G., & McDonald, D. A. (2010). A critical review of public-public partnerships in water services. *Water Alternatives*, *3*(1), 1–25.

Budds, J., & McGranahan, G. (2003). Are the debates on water privatization missing the point? Experiences from Africa, Asia and Latin America. *Environment & Urbanization*, *15*(2), 87–114. https://doi.org/10.1177/0956247803015000222

Castree, N. (2008). Neoliberalising nature: Processes, effects, and evaluations. *Environment and Planning A: Economy and Space*, *40*(1), 153–173. https://doi.org/10.1068/a39100

Castro, J. (2009). Systemic conditions and public policy in the water and sanitation sector. In J. Castro & L. Heller (Eds.), *Water and sanitation services: Public policy and management* (pp. 19–37). Earthscan.

Conaghan, C. M., & Malloy, J. M. (1994). *Unsettling statecraft: Democracy and neoliberalism in the central Andes*. University of Pittsburgh Press.

Devine, F. (1995). Qualitative analysis. In D. Marsh & G. Stoker (Eds.), *Theory and methods in political science*. MacMillan.

Driessen, T. (2008). Collective management strategies and elite resistance in Cochabamba, Bolivia. *Development*, *51*, 89–95.

Estrin, S., & Pelletier, A. (2018). Privatization in developing countries: What are the lessons of recent experience? *The World Bank Research Observer*, *33*(1), 65–102. https://doi.org/10.1093/wbro/lkx007

Franceys, R., & Weitz, A. (2003). Public: Private community partnerships in infrastructure for the poor. *Journal of International Development*, *15*(8), 1083–1098. https://doi.org/10.1002/jid.1052

Hall, D., & Lobina, E. (2007). Profitability and the poor: Corporate strategies, innovation and sustainability. *Geoforum*, *38*(5), 772–785. https://doi.org/10.1016/j.geoforum.2006.08.012

Howell, J., & Pearce, J. (2001). *Civil society & development: A critical exploration.* L. Rienner Publishers.

Kishimoto, S., & Petitjean, O. (Eds.). (2017). *Reclaiming public services: How cities and citizens are turning back privatisation.* Transnational Institute.

Kishimoto, S., Steinfort, L., & Petitjean, O. (2020). *The future is public.* Transnational Institute.

Kohl, B. (2002). Stabilizing neoliberalism in Bolivia: Popular participation and privatization. *Political Geography*, *21*, 449–472.

Lobina, E. (2017). Water remunicipalisation: Between pendulum swings and paradigm advocacy. In S. Bell, A. Allen, P. Hofmann, & T.-H. Teh (Eds.), *Urban water trajectories* (pp. 149–161). Springer International Publishing.

McDonald, D. A. (2016). *Making public in a privatized world: The struggle for essential services.* ZED Books.

McDonald, D. A. (2018). Remunicipalization: The future of water services? *Geoforum*, *91*(Complete), 47–56. https://doi.org/10.1016/j.geoforum.2018.02.027

McDonald, D. A. (2019). Finding common(s) ground in the fight for water remunicipalization. *Community Development Journal*, *54*(1), 59–79. https://doi.org/10.1093/cdj/bsy054

McDonald, D. A., Marois, T., & Barrowclough, D. (2020). *Public banks and COVID-19: Combatting the pandemic with public finance.* Municipal Services Project; UNCTAD; Eurodad.

McDonald, D. A., & Ruiters, G. (2012). *Alternatives to privatization: Public options for essential services in the Global South.* Routledge.

Paulson, S., & Gezon, L. L. (Eds.). (2005). *Political ecology across spaces, scales, and social groups.* Rutgers University Press.

Pigeon, M., McDonald, D. A., Hoedeman, O., & Kishimoto, S. (2012). *Remunicipalisation: Putting water back into public hands.* Transnational Institute.

Sick, D. (2008). Social contexts and consequences of institutional change in common-pool resource management. *Society & Natural Resources*, *21*(2), 94–105. https://doi.org/10.1080/08941920701681524

Smith, D. E. (2007). Institutional ethnography: From a sociology for women to a sociology for people. In S. N. Hesse-Biber (Ed.), *Handbook of feminist research: Theory and praxis.* SAGE Publications.

Snow, D., & Trom, D. (2002). The case study and the study of social movements. In B. Klandermans & S. Staggenborg (Eds.), *Methods of social movement research.* University of Minnesota Press.

Spronk, S. (2010). Water and sanitation utilities in the Global South: Re-centering the debate on "efficiency". *Review of Radical Political Economics, 42*(2), 156–174. https://doi.org/10.1177/0486613410368389

Swyngedouw, E. (1997). Power, nature, and the city: The conquest of water and the political ecology of urbanization in Guayaquil, Ecuador: 1880–1990. *Environment and Planning A, 29*(2), 311–332.

Swyngedouw, E. (2005). Dispossessing H2O: The contested terrain of water privatization. *Capitalism, Nature, Socialism, Abingdon, 16*(1), 81–98. http://dx.doi.org.proxy.queensu.ca/10.1080/1045575052000335384

Swyngedouw, E. (2007). Technonatural revolutions: The scalar politics of Franco's hydro-social dream for Spain, 1939–1975. *Transactions of the Institute of British Geographers, 32*(1), 9–28. https://doi.org/10.1111/j.1475-5661.2007.00233.x

Villena Villegas, F. (2009). *Sonqo rimarej Decires del Corazon*. Plural editors.

Yeboah, I. (2006). Subaltern strategies and development practice: Urban water privatization in Ghana. *Geographical Journal, 172*(1), 50–65. https://doi.org/10.1111/j.1475-4959.2006.00184.x

2 Protracted water crisis in the garden city

I think Semapa's services improved, although there is much left to do. We still suffer from water rationing. The frequency of water delivery favours those connected to the network. Hopefully things improve in such a way that we all can see the battle in April was not in vain.

—Resident ("Semapa dice que la etapa difícil ya paso," 19 October 2000)[1]

When do we stop believing in false promises? When will the water reach the Southern Zone?

—Resident, District 14 (9 August 2016, Water Summit)

The two foregoing quotes from water users—separated by 16 years—are telling of both the promise and the frustration of water services in Cochabamba, Bolivia. The first water user was quoted a few months after the Water War, at the peak of the water movement's drive to repair Cochabamba's broken system after the failed privatization. The second laments the status of service after a decade and a half of public sector reform. Cochabamba's "David versus Goliath" battle over privatized water services garnered international attention, and the case is upheld as a victory and a pivotal moment of resistance against privatization forces (Assies, 2003). Yet nearly two decades later, the public water operator that replaced it still does not adequately provide for all Cochabamba residents.

By the late 1990s, slated as a dysfunctional, inefficient service, Cochabamba's municipal water provider, Semapa, was targeted for privatization. Water services had been one of the few sectors to escape the climate of neoliberal privatization that swept the country (and the continent as a whole) in that decade. Neoliberal structural adjustment policies based on economic liberalization, minimal state intervention, and the free flow of goods and capital were imposed in Bolivia as part of the World Bank's conditions for external debt repayment (Kohl & Farthing, 2009; Veltmeyer & Tellez,

DOI: 10.4324/9781003169383-2

2001). The privatization of water systems followed the logic that determining the true market price of water results in a more efficient system by creating a monetary incentive for water conservation, based on the assumption that profit-seeking companies are more accountable to customers and shareholders (Nickson & Vargas, 2002). Laws were promulgated to facilitate the sale of public water utilities, and, in 1999, Semapa became Aguas del Tunari, a subsidiary of the US-based multinational corporation Bechtel. A point hotly debated and contested in Cochabamba was that the contract granted the private company monopoly rights to all infrastructure and water sources within the concession zone, which included informal small-scale water systems and water sources used by irrigating farmers. Skyrocketing tariffs that did not correspond to improved services served to strengthen the resistance to privatization (Olivera & Lewis, 2004).

Emboldened through *La Coordinadora* (Coalition for the Defence of Water and Life—*Coordinadora por la Defensa del Agua y la Vida*), a grassroots coalition, people took to the streets by the thousands in early April 2000 to reject the commercialization of water and demand the restoration of water services to public hands. "*El agua es nuestro carajo*" ("the water is ours, dammit") was the battle cry that resonated throughout the region and internationally, signalling the popular frustration with neoliberal policies that pushed marginalized factions of society further towards the edge (Olivera & Lewis, 2004). Central demands of the water movement included the dissolution of the private contract, reversal of the privatization law, and the democratization of water governance via social control and public participation. Under pressure from unrelenting protests and despite violent police suppression, the government of President Hugo Banzer was forced to cancel the contract with Aguas del Tunari in early April 2000 (for excellent accounts of the historical event see Olivera & Lewis, 2004, Crespo et al., 2004; see and Bustamante et al., 2005; Laurie, 2011 for gender analyses).

The Water War of 2000 in Cochabamba was a catalyst for further anti-privatization movements in Bolivia, leading to the second Water War of 2005 and the Gas Wars of 2003 and 2005 in La Paz-El Alto, fuelled by demands for broader public control of natural resources (Dangl, 2007; Perreault, 2005). In the end, the short-lived water privatization attempt in Cochabamba unequivocally failed, rendering this water management model untenable in the future, both legally and in the collective consciousness. The water company reverted to Semapa, under control of the municipal government. However, attempts to overhaul the company and democratize water management have been largely unsuccessful since then. As a result, the city of Cochabamba continues to suffer a prolonged water crisis.

This book examines the aftermath of the Cochabamba Water War—in terms of how the momentum of that event was harnessed at the time and altered over the years—in an effort to understand why public water restructuring has not met the goals it set for itself post-privatization. This chapter provides a broad overview of water issues in Cochabamba before delving into the concepts of social control and participation that were, and remain, central to the public water movement. I use the concept of a hydrosocial cycle (Linton & Budds, 2014) to understand how water is produced and distributed and to demonstrate the complexity of Cochabamba's urban waterscape. Following the flow of water allows us to trace constraints and tensions around water provision and to provide a physical sense of the area's water basin.

Stemming from a political ecology tradition, the concept of a *hydrosocial* cycle emerged as a critical response to the traditional scientific *hydrological* cycle that abstracts water processes from social and political dynamics. Conversely, the hydrosocial cycle conceives of water as a socionatural hybrid that embodies material, discursive, and symbolic processes (Swyngedouw, 2004). This concept is useful as a framework to examine how everyday water practices in Cochabamba are differentiated and inform broader political processes and consolidations of power. Tracing the water flow from water sources, water infrastructure, the tap/household, and, finally, wastewater infrastructure and disposal, I will highlight the power dynamics embedded in the Cochabamba waterscape.

Water sources

Nestled in the Cochabamba Valley along the semi-arid Andean plateau at 2,500 m above sea level, the city of Cochabamba (from the Quechua *Kocha Pampa*, loosely translating to "Land of Lakes") was named for its abundance of water. Cochabamba was historically a highly agriculturally productive centre, and people are attracted to the garden city for its mild climate. These monikers are now less apt due to diminishing agriculture and perpetual drought, in part due to rapid urbanization that has slowed the rate of aquifer recharge during the short 70-day rainy season (Ledo, 2013). The Cochabamba Valley as a whole suffers from water deficit.

Another complicating factor is that Semapa's main water supply (from ground and surface waters) lies outside its political jurisdiction. The most important reservoirs are Escalerani and Wara Wara in the neighbouring municipalities of Tiquipaya and Sacaba, which account for approximately 30% of Semapa's water which covers service in the Centre and North districts of Cochabamba. Semapa also relies on groundwater from controversial deep well drilling and, most recently, on water from Misicuni, a scandal-ridden multipurpose dam project under construction since the 1960s located 35 km northwest of the city. Table 2.1 provides an overview

Figure 2.1 Map of South America
Credit: Ashley Rudy.

of water sources used by Semapa, excluding wells drilled in and outside of the Cochabamba area that are no longer operational.

An estimated two thirds of the city's population is supplied with groundwater (Ledo, 2013). The use of water wells by communities and on private lots is prolific and unregulated, contributing to the overexploitation of aquifers. Another challenge is that the Southern Zone of Cochabamba (forming

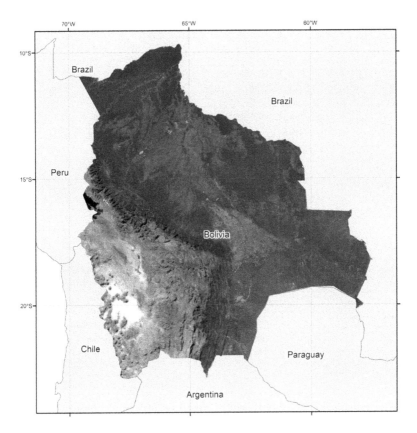

Figure 2.2 Map of Bolivia

Credit: Ashley Rudy.

the poorest parts of the city) is largely not connected to Semapa's water infrastructure. Instead, autonomous, self-governed small-scale community providers, known as water committees and water cooperatives, supply water from their own wells or purchase from water trucks, *aguateros*, which provide a middle-man service delivering water sourced from approximately 40 privately owned wells in the northern districts of the city, built on residential lots.

There are approximately 5,000–7,000 small water wells in the metropolitan region (Assies, 2003). Pervasive drilling has long been a source of conflict in Bolivia due to limited volumes of water (Bustamante et al., 2005). To combat the water shortage plaguing the city of Cochabamba, Semapa drilled wells in the neighbouring town of Quillacollo, first in the

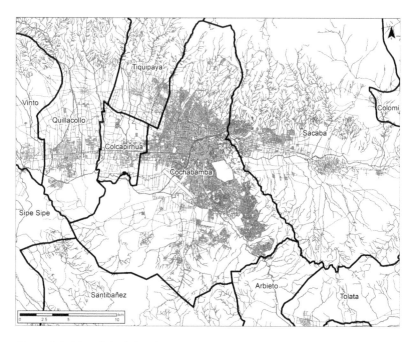

Figure 2.3 City of Cochabamba
Credit: Ashley Rudy.

1970s and again in the 1990s. These initially short-term drilling solutions dried up nearby community wells, leading to a series of conflicts between Semapa and irrigating farmers in 1998 known as *Guerra de los Pozos*—War of the Wells (Assies, 2003). Importantly, these events led to the formation of the federation of irrigating farmers, FEDECOR (Cochabamba Department Federation of Irrigators' Organization) whose members equipped them-selves with knowledge of water legislation. These experiences shaped FEDECOR, which later played a key role during the Water War of 2000, fighting for public control of water systems.

Communal irrigation systems originally created by Quechua and Aymara peoples survived Spanish colonization and remained through the 1953 Agrarian Reform that initiated the redistribution of land from landlords to peasants (Zimmerer, 2000). Farming communities continue to access the water based upon usufruct rights, a form of collective management that grants access to water "in turn" based on social agreements negotiated and renegotiated over time, known as *usos y costumbres*—uses and customs (Boelens & Hoogendam, 2002; Bustamante et al., 2005).

Table 2.1 Semapa water sources

Type of water	Name/Information	Location/ Municipality	Volume to Semapa (m3/year)
Groundwater	Vinto Ten deep wells drilled in 1977. Eight are functional; currently only four are operational.	Vinto	1,200,890
	Paso I Various wells drilled from 1974–5. Due to high levels of iron and soil degradation, only 1 well is operational in Coña Coña. In el Paso, near the Khora River there are 7 operational wells.	Quillacollo	11,006,064
	Paso II Several wells drilled from 1994–5 with international cooperation. Only 2 are operational.		
	Paso III Four operational wells, drilled in 2001.		
	Colquiri, Condebamba, Santa Ana, Melchor, La Pajcha, Alamos y Asociados. Wells within the city built in different years that serve isolated networks. Two are no longer operational.	Central Cochabamba (Colquiri, Condebamba, Santa Ana, Melchor, La Pajcha, Alamos y Asociados)	494,484
		Subtotal Groundwater: 12,701,439	
Surface water	Escalerani system	Tiquipaya	7,603,644
	Wara Wara System	Sacaba	1,508,997
	Chungara	Cercado	652,479
	Arocagua	Cercado	597,922
	Misicuni	Quillacollo	7,089,608
		Subtotal Surface water: 17,452,653	
		Total Sources: 30, 154,092	

(Data from Semapa, 2011; MMAyA, 2013, pp. 5–6)

The defence of *usos y costumbres* became a driving force and organizing strategy invoked against water privatization in Cochabamba (Crespo et al., 2004). Though they did not receive their drinking water from the city supplier, irrigating farmers were concerned about the private contract with Aguas del Tunari because it granted the company monopoly rights to all water sources and related infrastructures within the concession zone. Further, the Law on Potable Water and Sewage (No. 2029) introduced licenses and concessions, for a period of 40 years, for institutions with legal status but favoured those that adhered to market criteria. In essence, the law legalized the privatization contract signed a few months prior to the law's enactment. The irrigators perceived the contract and law as a threat to their *usos y costumbres* because the exclusive rights to the concession zone granted to Aguas del Tunari meant access to water would now depend on contracts with the private company (Assies, 2003). Road barricades held by the irrigators during the Water War on the city outskirts were not eased until negotiations began to substantially modify Law 2029. The water committees and cooperatives in the Southern Zone, often overlooked by the government, joined in the water movement, as they shared similar concerns over the potential appropriation of their water systems. In this regard, the protests can be viewed as a defence of the commons against capital encroachment (Spronk & Webber, 2007). Linked to the fight for water and crucial to the livelihood of the communities within and outside of Cochabamba is the broader question of ownership and decision-making power in natural resource management (Crespo, 2006).

Major political shifts occurred in Bolivia in the years following the Water War of 2000. Building momentum and support from the water mobilization, the Movement Towards Socialism (MAS) shifted to form a political party and Evo Morales was elected to office as the first Indigenous president in 2005 (taking office in early 2006). Some of the first major changes Morales made corresponded to the demands of actors in the water movement, including the creation of a new Water Ministry and corresponding institutions, establishing water as a fundamental human right, banning the commercialization of water, and, importantly, the legal recognition of *usos y costumbres* and community water providers. FEDECOR achieved a symbolic victory with a sectorial irrigation law that heavily cites *usos y costumbres* (Perreault, 2008). According to the new Constitution (EPA, 2009), all water is under public (read state) jurisdiction, though management by communities under *usos y costumbres* is recognized. Though historically constrained by state law, peasant and Indigenous communities in the Andes view the law as an important resource to defend collective water rights (Boelens, 2008).

For Cochabamba, the new laws and policies cancelled the threat of water privatization from foreign capital and highlighted the plight of small-scale community systems in the Southern Zone. However, the coalition of different sectors that united during the Water War weakened over the years, and pre-existing tensions between city and country eventually re-emerged. As sociologist Sonia Dávila-Poblete puts it, "all conflicts are latent" (Interview, Dávila-Poblete, 2014). For example, disputes have recently reignited in neighbouring municipalities over Semapa's exploitation of well water outside of the city of Cochabamba ("Avanza 1 de 4 ductos para Misicuni", 2016). The question of water access and ownership remains extremely contentious, exacerbated by limited watershed coordination across different sectors, lack of an updated overarching water law, and chronic drought (Durán, 2012).[2]

The consequences of climate change are exacerbating waterscape tensions in Cochabamba as well, with shorter, more intense periods of rainfall and longer periods of drought contributing to hydraulic stress (Semapa, 2011). Surface waters have seen a reduction in volume with an increased rate of evaporation, while groundwater is not being replenished at the same rate, due in part to overexploitation and shrinking glaciers in the nearby mountains (Semapa, 2011). Rising temperatures and precipitation changes resulted in glacial retreat of 30% surface area from 1970–2006 in Bolivia (Hicks & Fabricant, 2016, p. 139). These climatic changes have wreaked havoc on the country's important water bodies; for example, Lake Poopo (located in Oruro Department) completely disappeared in 2017, while torrential rainfall in the eastern Amazon region devastated communities. In Cochabamba, cycles of intense drought put the city on crisis alert in the winter months of 2016. However, as the next section will elucidate, water scarcity provides a convenient narrative to excuse flaws in the infrastructure.

Water infrastructure in Cochabamba

From the reservoirs, water is conducted through a series of dams, tunnels, canals, and pipes, often traversing large distances to reach the treatment plants (Cala, Aranjuez, and Taquiña) and storage tanks (groundwater is most often chlorine-treated in tanks). The water is then pumped through the city's distribution network to reach water users. Inadequate infrastructure in Cochabamba is a main factor contributing to uneven access to water resources. Cochabamba's water services are extremely heterogeneous, with people's everyday interactions with water varying greatly depending on location. In 1994, a decentralization policy divided the city into 14 districts (Ledo, 2005). The Northern and Central Zones of the city (composed of districts 1, 2, 3, 4, and 13), which generally hold more economic power, are supplied by Semapa. Most of the more marginalized Southern Zone (composed of districts 5, 6, 7, 8, 9, and 14) is generally not directly connected to the public network (see Figure 2.4).

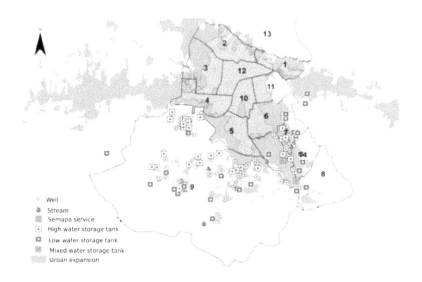

Figure 2.4 Water provision by zone

Credit: Adapted from (Semapa, 2011).

Semapa, the municipal water company, was established in 1967, after the city had shifted towards an economy based on commerce, small-scale industry, and services, and it was designed to service a population of roughly 200,000. Falling tin prices and the closure of tin mines in the 1980s occasioned a mass migration that saw Cochabamba's population explode to half a million by the mid-1990s. Cochabamba is now the fourth largest city in Bolivia with a population of over 600,000 (INE, 2014). New migrants settled in the city's peripheral districts in the Southern Zone in self-made homes in areas lacking in basic services (Ledo, 2013). Rapid urbanization was not matched by corresponding water infrastructure. Today, Semapa's 75,000 residential and commercial water connections reach just over 350,000 people. But even here Semapa's service is notoriously uneven and intermittent, unable to provide water 24 hours per day to citizens that are connected to the network. In times of drought, Semapa's water rationing means distribution can be reduced to once a week. Semapa's Client Service Department receives up to 1,000 complaints per month from dissatisfied water users (Amurrio Montes, 2017).

The variability in water availability is primarily due to an obsolete distribution network, with an estimated 46% water loss due to leakages, compared to a 27% water loss in the Santa Cruz (Bolivia) water system (Semapa, 2011).

The network pipes in the *casco viejo*, the old centre of the city, are over 50 years old and in a state of "complete deterioration," with displaced or deteriorated joints that allow infiltration, sedimentation, and clandestine domestic connections (MMAyA, 2013, pp. 3–42). Together, this results in large volumes of unaccounted water losses and contamination. Over the years, Semapa representatives and municipal government officials (from different political parties) have used water scarcity to explain the lack of universal access. Though depleted water sources have an important impact, at least one local water engineer calculates that the volume lost through leakages would meet the needs of the entire population (Interview, Rodriguez, 2014).

The infrastructure problems are long-standing and date to the period before the Water War. Proponents of water privatization inside and outside of Bolivia pointed to inefficiency in the publicly run service as the primary cause of the deteriorated system. In their view, a private company, more accountable to customers and shareholders, could achieve the necessary infrastructure improvements and expand services through cost recovery (Nickson & Vargas, 2002). However, these changes did not materialize under the brief privatization period, and since 2000 the improvements to infrastructure have been piecemeal, including regular maintenance work and expansions in the northern part of the city (Interview, Semapa worker, 2014). From 2006 to 2014, drinking water coverage increased by 7.7%, with an additional 9,000 connections to the Semapa network (Semapa, 2014). Yet major infrastructure projects to replace the *casco viejo* network and expand service to the Southern Zone have been repeatedly impeded by funding obstacles. Securing loans following the Water War was complicated by Semapa's institutional debt, problems of corruption, disputes among water sector actors, and, not least, by strict conditions imposed by international financial institutions (Sánchez Gómez & Terhorst, 2005). Most recently a major adduction line was completed in collaboration with Japanese cooperation, ostensibly connecting the Semapa network to southern districts, yet—partially due to insufficient community input in planning—the infrastructure does not function at full capacity.

In the absence of state support, communities in the Southern Zone districts organized to build water systems self-governed through water committees, water cooperatives, or territorial organizations, starting in the 1980s (Walnycki, 2020). There now are approximately 200 of these small-scale providers in the southern periphery whose access to water can be precarious. Many rely on community wells that often do not produce enough water or are too saline or contaminated to use safely. Some water committees and cooperatives have agreements to purchase water in bulk from Semapa; this is commonly referred to as co-management, though all decision-making and costs of water administration remain within the community, with Semapa simply supplying the liquid. Other systems rely on *aguateros* to deliver water, which is more expensive and of unregulated quality.

The oldest of the small-scale system networks were built with community member contributions of money and labour using any materials and knowledge available. After the Water War, the plight of small-scale providers was brought to light, and this heightened visibility translated to a flood of external assistance from NGOs and government (Interview, Ledo, 2014). Though this funding contributes to maintenance of the community systems, uneven and sometimes chaotic distribution of funds over time and across communities impacts the quality of the networks and service. The sustainability of each system is variable, as some groups have a greater capacity to maintain their networks, while others are dealing with aging networks.

A new Water and Sanitation Law (No. 2066) permits water committees and cooperatives to register as formal water providers for their communities. As Ekers and Loftus (2008) point out, legitimacy is often linked to government institutions. By engaging with the state legal system, which they previously existed outside of, small-scale providers can gain greater legitimacy to secure the autonomy and survival of their systems, which are viewed by some actors as second-rate, provisional services. The formal recognition of these providers that function within Semapa's jurisdiction also leads to confusion over the responsibility for water provision. The future of these systems remains a point of contention in the Cochabamba water sector that feeds into the uneasy relations between the different city districts.

Tap/Household

The city of Cochabamba represents 60% of the metropolitan population, which consumes 70% of the available freshwater (Ledo, 2013). According to Semapa data, the average consumer uses 137 litres per person per day (Semapa, 2014, p. 13). Residences in the North and Centre have storage tanks that can typically store 1,000 litres of water over two days, meaning that families can ration water when Semapa is not delivering daily. Water quality is poor due to contamination incurred through infrastructure, and there is an unofficial permanent boil advisory. Boiling water to bathe newborns is a common method used by mothers to avoid disease (Interview, Water user, 2014). Due to the limited quantity of water and potential health risks, wealthier households that receive Semapa water typically supplement the tap water with bottled water. Despite the water rationing, there is no established culture of conservation in the Northern and Central Zones where water is nevertheless more readily available. Potable water used to irrigate domestic and public gardens, clear asphalt paths and sidewalks, and wash cars can be regularly observed.

In the Southern Zone, faced with the challenge of extremely limited water, potable water goes through several cycles of use as many residents repurpose it to bathe, clean, and irrigate. Collection of rainwater is also a common strategy in several communities. Water quality for neighbourhoods not connected to the municipal system varies depending on the source of crude water. Water committees and cooperatives contend with the drying up of wells and contamination from nearby industrial waste. There is little quality control for water delivered by *aguateros*, much of which is contaminated en route, and water users complain of bugs and germs forming as the water sits in storage barrels for days. Ledo (2013) recounts a case of women in the Southern Zone who designed innovative methods to treat saline water from wells. These strategies highlight the resourcefulness of the women but also point to the additional gendered burden they face dealing with water quality issues.

At the household level, water users contend with the costs of water services. Water tariffs remain a highly contested issue since the Water War. Law 2029, which legalized privatization, also contained criteria to establish cost-recovery tariffs to capitalize the private company. This led to dramatic spikes in tariffs that were unaffordable for most Cochabamba citizens and spurred even middle- and upper-income residents of the North and Centre of the city to mobilize against Aguas del Tunari. Since the Water War, ongoing debates about Semapa nearly always involve the tariff structure. Low tariffs are blamed for the inability to fund service improvements, yet tariffs have been raised steadily over the years and continue to be a source of frustration (Interview, Crespo, 2014).

The same pre-privatization tariff categorization system is still in place, dividing residential users into four categories[3] based on building type, plot size, construction condition, and the number of water points (faucets). The differentiated rates mean that the tariffs increase as the house size and number of water points increase. A minimum tariff applies to the first 0–12 m^3 (a flat rate of 18 bolivianos[4] per month for the lowest category and up to 113 Bolivanos for the highest category), charged regardless of the amount of water consumed (Semapa, 2018). The rate for cubic metres of water consumed beyond the first 12 m^3 increases only incrementally; therefore, higher levels of consumption are not heavily penalized. As Ledo (2013) points out, this relatively flat tariff system favours the highest income groups that consume the greatest volume of available water. Furthermore, many residential homes are not properly categorized by the municipality, so many upgraded homes are still being charged at the lowest rates, effectively nullifying any progressive subsidy structure (Ledo, 2013). In any case, these rates only apply to Semapa users in the North and Centre of the city. For poorer residents in the Southern Zone not connected to the municipal

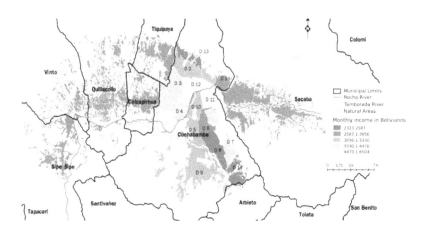

Figure 2.5 Income distribution

Credit: Adapted from Juan E. Cabrera, ERM, & Sebastián Lew, 2013.

service or small-scale water systems, water is often purchased via *agua-teros* that charge upwards of 7 bolivianos per 0.2 m³ barrel of water. This means that some of the most marginalized populations are paying the highest prices for water. Figures 2.6 and 2.7 illustrate this disparity between access to water and income distribution.

Another key contention with the Semapa tariff system regards old meters that capture air pressure as water used and thereby artificially inflate consumption levels, a continuous complaint among users. Furthermore, the sewage fee is 40% of the total rate for water consumption, which drives up the bill substantially (Ledo, 2013). For those without meters, bills are estimated according to the consumption of metered users within the same category. Residents lament the high cost of water during the rationing of service, for water that is not delivered. For years, citizens have been demanding a system to pay according to the actual volume of water consumed.

In October 2016 Semapa presented a new tariff structure proposal during one of the city's worst droughts. The proposal eliminated subcategories for residential[5] based on housing, instead establishing rates according to volume of water consumed monthly. A residential "solidarity" rate charges 10 bolivianos for 0–3 m³ and a basic domestic rate of 20 bolivianos for 4–6 m³, 5 bolivianos for every additional cubic metre, and 10 bolivianos for every cubic meter consumed over 30 m³ (Meza Tiga, 2016). The new structure ostensibly provided an incentive for more careful water

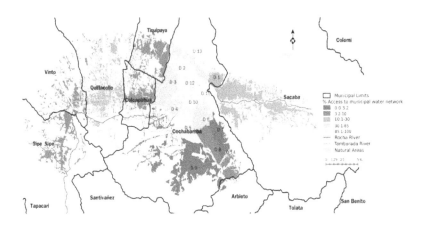

Figure 2.6 Access to municipal water services

Adapted from Juan E. Cabrera, ERM, & Sebastián Lew, 2013.

consumption. However, critics immediately pointed to key flaws in the proposal: the volumes of water suggested by Semapa of 0–4 m³ (under the solidarity and basic categories) meet basic access standards, yet the World Health Organization categorizes the low volumes as posing low to high health risks (Campanini, 2016). Further, the proposed solidarity tariff represents double the solidarity tariffs of other major Bolivian cities. Five years on, Semapa's administration has effectively halted the implementation of the solidarity tariff, saying that the 2016 tariff calculations no longer correspond with water prices and maintenance costs and are thus unsustainable ("Semapa paraliza nuevas tarifas", 2021).

This decision fuels the general mistrust that the state will act in the community's best interests (Zibechi, 2009). Many neighbourhoods in the Southern Zone reject the idea of relinquishing their community systems to the municipal-run network, particularly for fear of increased tariffs. The smaller scale of water committees and cooperatives provides participatory spaces where members collectively agree on affordable pricing and can decide to offer differentiated rates to community members in need (a difficult task for the heavily bureaucratic and centralized Semapa institution). The downside of these typically low-cost services, however, is limited income that can be directed towards network maintenance or emergencies (see Table 2.2 for tariff comparison). The severe droughts experienced by Cochabamba mean that more small-scale systems in the South rely on *aguateros* to fulfil their water requirements, whose prices have since surged.

Table 2.2 Comparative cost of water by provider

Provider	Cost per m³ (bolivianos)
Semapa	18 for the first 0–12 m³
Community systems	1–7 (variable tariff structures)
Aguateros	25–100

Other formats (commercial)	*Cost per litre (bolivianos)*
2 L Disposable water bottle	2.5
6 L Disposable water bottle (Coca-Cola)	2.5
20 L Returnable water bottle	0.85

Wastewater infrastructure and disposal

Semapa has approximately 83,000 sewage connections to its main treatment plant, which serve 41% of the population (Semapa presentation; MMAyA, 2013). This figure is higher than the potable water connections, because certain neighbourhoods combine Semapa sewage service with their community governed water systems. Figure 2.6 illustrates Semapa's sewage coverage and indicates regions where community sewage networks are not in use because they are not connected to the main sewage pipelines. A 2004 study revealed that parts of the sewage network in the *casco viejo* collapsed or completely deteriorated as a result of hydrogen sulfide from wastewater, contributing to aquifer contamination (MMAyA, 2013, pp. 3–96). The Northern and Central Zones of Cochabamba are covered for residual water collection; however, many of the pipes are nearing their shelf life and need to be replaced, a complicated process in the older sections of the city.

Wastewater infrastructure in the Southern Zone is more limited. Semapa services some neighbourhoods through smaller stations in varying conditions (good to poor) that pump water to Cochabamba's main wastewater treatment facility, Albarrancho (MMAyA, 2013). During the rainy season, it is not uncommon for these small stations to overflow. Groundwater is vulnerable to contamination at a higher rate due to the absence of a sewage system in large parts of the Southern Zone and due to the prevalence of septic tanks and latrines. Further contributing factors to contamination include commercial and industrial chemicals, leaching garbage, and cast-off from agricultural and livestock farming (MMAyA, 2013, pp. 3–51). Many community wells are no longer usable due to the high levels of contamination.

The then director of Albarrancho, the wastewater treatment plant, attested that Semapa regularly does not meet the permissible limits determined through Bolivian legislation (Interview, Albarrancho Director, 2014). Located in the southeast portion of Cochabamba near the airport,

Albarrancho was completed in 1986 and, like the water infrastructure, was designed to serve a much smaller population. With a capacity of treating 400 L/s of sewage, Albarrancho is not equipped to treat the 800 L/s that it currently receives (Interview, Albarrancho director, 2014). This means that wastewater exits Albarrancho untreated, contributing to the contamination of the Rocha and Tamborada rivers. The Rocha River that flows through Cochabamba is called the "Black Serpent" by locals due to further pollution from commercial and domestic garbage as well as improper use for laundry and car washes. Nevertheless, downstream from the Albarrancho plant, people use the contaminated Rocha River water for agricultural irrigation (Interview, Albarrancho Director, 02014). Because of the perceived urgency of the water intake situation, less attention and resources are focused on the wastewater contamination, which represents a "real environmental catastrophe at the doorstep of the city of Cochabamba" (MMAyA, 2013, pp. 3–98).

Conclusion

This overview of the waterscape of Cochabamba reveals that far from achieving universal water access since the Water War, the city of Cochabamba still suffers grave water problems. Cochabamba's water service has been characterized as a "precarious and class-based distribution of a scarce collective consumption good" (Assies, 2003, p. 21). This characterization remains valid over a decade and a half later, as the hydrosocial cycle exposes power asymmetries corresponding to relative privilege. The notion of water scarcity serves to obscure fundamental problems of unequal distribution. In referring to Cochabamba's "parallel networks" (Bakker, 2010) or labelling Cochabamba as a "dual city" (Ledo, 2013), researchers emphasize this dichotomy in water access.

In general terms, the interests of the city's wealthy are better served than those of the poor. At the same time, the existing water provision by Semapa is, at best, the same as the pre-privatization period, with chronic water shortages and quality control problems. The shift in government as MAS took power nationally resulted in new legislative and policy directions in the water sector based on demands that originated in the Water War, yet their implementation has been slow to materialize into concrete changes locally. Why has it been so difficult to rebuild a successful public service? This is the question at the heart of the book, to which I now turn.

Notes

1 All Spanish text translated by the author.
2 For a regional historical approach to water governance in Cochabamba, see Sarah T. Hines (2021) *Water for all: Community, property, and revolution in modern Bolivia.*

3 A different set of rates applies to categories of commercial, industrial, prefer-ential, and social. Semapa introduced a solidarity tariff in 2011 geared towards non-profits offering social services to vulnerable populations.
4 1 USD converts to 6.90 bolivianos (October 2021).
5 Other consumer categories of commercial, industrial, preferential, and social users are charged a fixed rate.
Dr. Ashley Rudy created the maps in Figures 2.1, 2.2, and 2.3.

References

Amurrio Montes, L. (2017, October 26). Hay mil reclamos al mes por falta de agua en Semapa. *Los Tiempos*.
Assies, W. (2003). David versus Goliath in Cochabamba. *Latin American Perspectives*, *30*(3), 14–36. https://doi.org/10.1177/0094582X03030003003
Avanza 1 de 4 ductos para Misicuni, Gobierno asegura que desde 2006 invirtió Bs 8.417 millones en proyectos de agua. *Los Tiempos*.
Bakker, K. J. (2010). *Privatizing water: Governance failure and the world's urban water crisis*. Cornell University Press.
Boelens, R. (2008). Water rights arenas in the Andes: Upscaling networks to strengthen local water control. *Water Alternatives*, *1*(1), 48–65.
Boelens, R., & Hoogendam, P. (2002). *Water rights and empowerment*. Uitgeverij Van Gorcum.
Bustamante, R., Peredo, E., & Udaeta, M. E. (2005). Women in the "water war" in the Cochabamba Valleys. In V. Bennett, S. Dávila-Poblete, & M. N. Rico (Eds.), *Opposing currents: The politics of water and gender in Latin America*. University of Pittsburgh Press. www.jstor.org/stable/j.ctt9qh61c
Cabrera, J. E., ERM, & Lew, S. (Cartographers). (2013). Plan de acción: Área met-ropolitana de Cochabamba sostenible. In M. V. Ortiz Echazú, L. F. Cabrera, & P. Zambrano Barragán (Eds.), *Iniciativa Ciudades emergentes y sostenibles*. Banco Interamericano de Desarrollo.
Campanini, O. (2016). *Crisis del agua y sequía en Bolivia*. CEDIB.
Crespo, C. F. (2006). *La ley de riego y sus reglamentos: Riesgos y desafíos: Vol. Boletín 78*. Comisión para la Gestión Integral del Agua en Bolivia (CGIAB).
Crespo, C. F., Peredo, C., & Omar, F. (2004). *Los regantes de Cochabamba en la guerra del agua: Presión social y negociación*. CESU-UMSS.
Dangl, B. (2007). *The price of fire: Resource wars and social movements in Bolivia*. AK Press.
Durán, A. (2012). Hacia una estrategia para la GIRH en Bolivia: Lecciones Apren-didas. In F. Quiroz, O. Delgadillo, & A. Durán (Eds.), *Aguas arriba, aguas abajo. Luces y sombras de la Gestión Integral de los Recursos Hídricos: Reflexiones desde la investigación aplicada* (pp. 445–464). Plural editores.
Ekers, M., & Loftus, A. (2008). The power of water: Developing dialogues between Foucault and gramsci. *Environment and Planning D: Society and Space*, *26*(4), 698–718. https://doi.org/10.1068/d5907
Estado Plurinacional de Bolivia [EPA]. (2009). *Nueva constitución política del estado*. UPS, La Paz.

Hicks, K., & Fabricant, N. (2016). The Bolivian climate justice movement. *Latin American Perspectives*, *43*(4), 87–104. https://doi.org/10.1177/0094582X16630308

Hines, S. T. (2021). *Water for all: Community, property, and revolution in modern Bolivia*. University of California Press.

INE (Instituto Nacional de Estadísticas), Estado Plurinacional de Bolivia. (2014). Censo Nacional de Población y Vivienda. *Statistics*. www.ine.gov.bo

Kohl, B., & Farthing, L. (2009). "Less than fully satisfactory development outcomes": International financial institutions and social unrest in Bolivia. *Latin American Perspectives*, *36*(3), 59–78. https://doi.org/10.1177/0094582X09334300

Laurie, N. (2011). Gender water networks: Femininity and masculinity in water politics in Bolivia. *International Journal of Urban and Regional Research*, *35*(1), 172–188. https://doi.org/10.1111/j.1468-2427.2010.00962.x

Ledo, C. (2005). *Inequality and access to water in the cities of Cochabamba and La Paz-El Alto*. United Nations Research Institute for Social Development.

Ledo, C. (2013). *El agua nuestra de cada día: Retos e iniciativas de una Cochabamba incluyente y solidaria*. CEPLAG-UMSS.

Linton, J., & Budds, J. (2014). The hydroscoial cycle: Defining and mobilizing a relational-dialectical approach to water. *Geoforum*, *57*, 170–180. https://doi.org/10.1016/j.geoforum.2013.10.008

Meza Tiga, S. (2016). La propuesta de Semapa baja precio del agua a la mitad. *Opinión*.

MMAyA. (2013). *Plan Maestro Metropolitano de Agua y Saneamiento del Area Metropolitano de Cochabamba*. Ministerio del Agua, Viceministerio de Riego.

Nickson, A., & Vargas, C. (2002). The limitations of water regulation: The failure of the Cochabamba concession in Bolivia. *Bulletin of Latin American Research*, *21*(1), 99–120.

Olivera, O., & Lewis, T. (2004). *¡Cochabamba!: Water war in Bolivia*. South End Press.

Opinión. (2000). Semapa dice que la etapa difícil ya paso. *Opinión*.

Perreault, T. (2005). State restructuring and the scale of rural water governance in Bolivia. *Environment and Planning A*, *37*(2), 263–284.

Perreault, T. (2008). Custom and contradiction: Rural water governance and the politics of Usos y Costumbres in Bolivia's irrigators' movement. *Annals of the Association of American Geographers*, *98*(4), 834–854. https://doi.org/10.1080/00045600802013502

Sánchez Gómez, L., & Terhorst, P. (2005). Cochabamba, Bolivia: Public-collective partnerships after the water war. In Balanya, Brennan, Hoedeman, Kishimoto, & P. Terhorst (Eds.), *Reclaiming public water: Achievements, struggles, and visions from around the world* (pp. 121–130). TNI.

Semapa. (2011). *Plan de desarrollo quinquenal 2012–2016*. Semapa.

Semapa. (2014). *Programa operativo annual: Gestión 2014*. Semapa.

Semapa. (2018). *Estructura tarifaria*. www.semapa.gob.bo/estructura-tarifaria

Semapa paraliza nuevas tarifas; no son sustentables. *Los Tiempos*. https://www.lostiempos.com/actualidad/cochabamba/20210803/semapa-paraliza-nuevas-tarifas-no-son-sustentables

Spronk, S., & Webber, J. R. (2007). Struggles against accumulation by dispossession in Bolivia: The political economy of natural resource contention. *Latin American Perspectives*, *34*(2), 31–47. https://doi.org/10.1177/0094582X06298748

Swyngedouw, E. (2004). *Social power and the urbanization of water: Flows of power*. Oxford University Press.

Veltmeyer, H., & Tellez, J. (2001). The state and participatory development in Bolivia. In *Transcending neoliberalism: Community-based development in Latin America* (pp. 64–94). Kumarian Press.

Walnycki, A. (2020). Rights on the edge of the city: Realizing the right to water in informal settlements in Bolivia. In F. Sultana & A. Loftus (Eds.), *Water politics: Governance, justice, and the right to water*. Routledge.

Zibechi, R. (2009). *Territorios En Resistencia*. Primera Edición en Bolivia.

Zimmerer, K. S. (2000). Rescaling irrigation in Latin America: The cultural images and political ecology of water resources. *Cultural Geographies*, *7*(2), 150–175. https://doi.org/10.1177/096746080000700202

3 What is social control? A typology of public participation in Bolivia

During the 2000 mobilization in Cochabamba, the water movement shared a vision of democratic water provision, framed by demands for social control (or *control social* in Spanish), a Bolivian term used in conjunction and sometimes interchangeably with public participation (*participación).* I contend in this chapter that the difficulty in rebuilding a strong public water service in Cochabamba partially stems from different—and often incompatible—understandings and interpretations of these concepts of public participation. Whose interests are served and which groups are included or excluded from access to water are tied to the question of public control over natural resources. In order to analyze the challenges to and opportunities for public participation in the remunicipalization of water in Cochabamba, it is important to first unpack the meanings, moments, and spaces of public participation in Bolivia more broadly.

The notion of public participation is now ubiquitous among development thinking and policy. A "warmly persuasive word" (Williams, 1976 in Hildyard et al., 2001, p. 58), participation has been heavily promoted and adopted in different circles over the past three decades. Difficulty in articulating a straightforward definition arises precisely because public participation is not a "single phenomenon" (Cohen & Uphoff, 1980, p. 34). A review of the international literature demonstrates its widespread use yet does not offer a consistent typology due to the concept's malleability to a spectrum of ideologies (Stiefel & Wolfe, 1994). This chapter seeks to lend conceptual clarity by developing a typology of different ways in which the term is used and how these differences manifest themselves in terms of intent. Specificity about meanings and practices of participation helps to adequately identify competing perspectives of public participation in Bolivia, which will be examined in general terms in this chapter in preparation for a more specific discussion of participation in water governance.

Broadly, public participation can be defined as engaging a wider cross-section of people or organizations in decision-making and/or implementation

DOI: 10.4324/9781003169383-3

of policy and services alongside controlling groups, presenting a shift away from exclusive or top-down processes. To examine participation, I utilize Cohen and Uphoff's (1980) concept of asking the following questions: participation by whom, for what, and in what? These questions lead to definitions that diverge dramatically into two overarching conceptualizations based on intentionality: participation as *reformative*, intended to modify decision-making processes without significantly changing the broader structures and ideologies of (market-based) power, and participation as *transformative*, intended to create a radical shift in social, economic, and institutional norms. A third form of participation exists that will be labelled as *nominal*, that is, a manipulation of the ideas and language of either of the foregoing forms in order to gain consent and legitimacy. The following section will review the conceptualization, intended outcome, actors, and key tools and practices of these forms of participation, as outlined in Table 3.1. The second half of this chapter will apply this framework to the Bolivian case. It should be noted that, while I draw on the extensive literature on the topic of participation and employ existing concepts, the typology laid out here is my own.

Reformative participation

The early 1990s marked the beginning of the "participatory turn" (Henkel et al., 2001) when participation became firmly established in mainstream development circles, commonly defined as "the process by which stakeholders influence and share control over priority setting, policy making, resource allocations, and/or program implementation" (WB, 2000, p. 237). The United Nations was particularly keen to incorporate popular participation into a wide range of its programmes, seeing it as "the organized efforts to increase control over resources and regulative institutions in given situations, on the part of groups and movements hitherto excluded from such control" (UNRISD Report cited in Stiefel & Wolfe, 1994, p. 5).

The label of *reformative participation* is apt because here participation is envisioned as a way to improve development in the face of partial market failure. These are partial failures in the sense that markets are seen to have brought about massive positive changes to the developing world but have missed important segments and sectors of society for a variety of reasons—one of which is identified as an imbalance of voice on the part of the poor. Persistent problems of inequity and poverty were attributed to traditional development practices of donor agencies delivering development solutions through large-scale, top-down, government-initiated programs. Re-orienting policies towards poverty reduction via "primary stakeholder participation" presented a way to address these asymmetries while remaining faithful to the dominant market-oriented development paradigm. Greater involvement of the poor and marginalized in

Table 3.1 Main elements of transformative, reformative, and nominal participation

Type of participation	Conceptualization	Intended outcome	Actors	Tools and practices
Reformative	Participation as a tool to create a fairer market-based economy and greater market-oriented competition by encouraging market access; development priorities not challenged beyond prescribed parameters. Participation occurs within official invited spaces.	Improve the situation within the context of market logic; further liberal agenda; improve development practices of agencies and professionals in order to better cope with existing structure; improve aid effectiveness by attaching "ownership" to projects.	International aid agencies; recipient governments; NGOs; end users or "primary stakeholders"	Community development; participatory learning and action/participatory rural appraisal; gender mainstreaming; decentralization; Poverty Reduction Strategy Paper (PRSP)
Transformative	Radically transform structures that reproduce poverty and marginalization; counter-hegemonic movement for social transformation; empowerment as exercising agency in decision-making, partaking in collective action. Participation can occur within structured pre-determined frameworks of change and/or within autonomous invented spaces.	Re-politicize participation; transform underlying forms of inequality and exclusion through redistribution of power; resistance to existing structure; empowerment (people make decisions/act for themselves).	Social movements; governments; NGOs	Participatory action research; collective action; participatory governance (e.g. Kerala, Porto Alegre, Oaxaca)

(*Continued*)

Table 3.1 (Continued)

Type of participation	Conceptualization	Intended outcome	Actors	Tools and practices
Nominal	Token form of participation used intentionally to gain consent and legitimacy for policy and practices; public relations exercise; participation is rhetorical, meaningful participation of little significance; can be adapted to any frame of reference. Participation necessarily occurs within official invited spaces.	Display; entrench status quo of power dynamics; appease opposition.	Used by institutions across the ideological spectrum in a variety of different socio-political contexts	Consultation; informing; manipulation of institutionalized mechanisms and laws

the policies that affect their lives would permit local people's knowledge to be at the centre of development planning, thus serving to ameliorate inequities and perceptions of injustice (see Cernea, 1991). This approach emphasizes the importance of local knowledge, shifting power towards "lowers" (the stakeholders) while the "uppers" (i.e. development experts) relinquish their professional prejudices and become facilitators of local knowledge (Chambers, 1994). The primary stakeholders are individuals who are "agents of development," and their "empowerment," the increased ability for individuals to pursue individual and collective goals, stems from increased participation in the free market economy (Kothari & Hickey, 2009; Leal, 2007). Importantly, however, people's empowerment does not shift the prevailing structural order or undermine the market economy (Mohan & Stokke, 2000).

Greater participation is seen as a way to enhance the market because it results in a better flow of information, more accountability, and greater competition. Participation can improve the flow of information from the "demand side," which results in greater market efficiency and effectiveness (Mansuri & Rao, 2013). Popular participation contributes inputs that form more "demand-driven" policies so that agencies can "re-orient towards the customers" (Long, 2001). In other words, it makes the corporations (aid agencies) more accountable to their customers (the poor). In turn, greater participation and accountability enhance market-based strategies by acting as a check and balance to the monopolization of power that exacerbates inequalities, as greater interaction with markets helps indicate where improvements can be made and accordingly diminishes practices that limit competition, such as collusion or price fixing. Crucially, the market is seen to produce opportunities, and participation is a way for disadvantaged groups to access these opportunities. Inclusion of the poor in the market through micro-credit or micro-financing schemes provides ways to create more economic activity and generate an environment conducive to an entrepreneurial class.

Proponents of this model of participation view any increased participation as an improvement. However, accepting as a forgone conclusion that macroeconomic stability and liberalizing markets are essential precludes any discussion of these that might occur as a result of participation. The outcome of development interventions would be improved by strengthening their legitimacy through local participation rather than by initiatives based solely on expert-knowledge. Funding community-level participatory projects through NGOs was viewed as beneficial or useful, as governments could pass off social services to NGOs and so-called project "transaction costs" to volunteer labour from within a community (Ackerman, 2004; Hildyard et al., 2001, p. 59). Encouraging self-management supported the disengagement with the interventionist state. Increasingly, a project's "effectiveness" and "sustainability" became linked to local participation (Long, 2001).

In these invited spaces, World Bank-supported policies and projects have a better chance of performing well, as participants have a stake in the project, often in the form of shared ownership. This dynamic is key to understanding the reformative nature of participation. People are granted agency but within prescribed parameters. The intended outcome of reformative participation is to modify development, correct imbalances, and increase opportunities for access that will ultimately enhance the market. Poverty reduction remains the focus, yet participatory practices do not question or confront the structural causes of poverty. Reformative participation adheres to the belief that poverty can be eradicated through market-oriented economic growth.

Proponents of reformative participation are chiefly international financial institutions interested in promulgating liberal economics. In a 2013 report, the World Bank boasted of 85 billion USD spent on local participatory development in the 2000s (Mansuri & Rao, 2013, p. ix). Governments that are aid recipients act to institutionalize the tools and practices of participation within their countries. The NGO sector has also played a role in implementation, as many NGOs advocate for participation as contributing to a more democratic development (Chambers, 2011; Long, 2001). Beneficiaries or primary stakeholders include the actors targeted under such participation schemes, typically poor and marginalized sectors of the population. Beneficiaries may choose to partake in participatory initiatives for the perceived benefits, utilize the tools to their advantage, and also abstain from and resist imposed participatory practices. Outlined below are some of the main tools and practices of reformative participation, including: community development, participatory learning and action/participatory rural appraisal, gender mainstreaming, and participatory governance.

Community development—The notion of community development first appeared in development interventions in the 1950s and 60s, yet these projects were eventually abandoned in favour of top-down technical approaches. The community approach to participation gained popularity once more during the 1990s and now forms part of many public sector endeavours. Generally, community development involves community members in the preparation and implementation of development projects, most often through "self-help labour" bestowed upon those without many resources (Chambers, 2011). This practice is purported to reinforce the sustainability of a project, as the people involved have invested their time and/or labour and have a vested interest in its success. However, during the phases of project development or monitoring and evaluation, community members' participation is not seen as vital (Long, 2001).

Participatory learning and action/participatory rural appraisal—Participatory learning and action (PLA) and the closely associated participatory rural appraisal (PRA) are amongst the most prominent and developed methods of reformative participation. As the participatory approach gained mainstream traction, PLA/PRA were ways to incorporate local knowledge into program planning, a way for the "unheard voices to be heard," yet they have lost their more radical connotations associated with participatory action research (Cornwall, 2003, p. 209). With less focus on the meaning of participation, demonstrating the involvement of beneficiaries became the marker of empowerment and success. PLA/PRA evolved into a set of easily quantifiable and measured practices and research methodologies that engage local voices and promote their influence (Mosse, 2003). The local knowledge accumulated from PLA/PRA practices is circumscribed to fit within the parameters of development interventions that have already been designed (Green, 2010). Further, in terms of addressing existing inequalities, PLA/PRA depends heavily on facilitators who may or may not have awareness of power and differences within communities (Cornwall, 2003).

Gender mainstreaming—Gender mainstreaming, which gained attention around the same time participatory practices were popularized, refers to a focus on gender in development policy and planning known as gender and development (GAD). While participatory practices do not always have an implicit gender focus (Cornwall, 1998; Crawley, 1998; Guijt & Shah, 1998), GAD does encourage greater participation of women in leadership roles in the public sphere, outside of traditional roles as wives/mothers in the private realm (Cornwall, 2003). This reformative approach also assumes empowerment and "heard voices" by virtue of including women. An example is setting quotas for women in politics as a form of participation.

Participatory governance—Participatory governance methods include, among other things: state–civic partnerships, democratic decentralization, participatory budgeting, citizens' hearings, and participatory poverty assessments (Hickey & Mohan, 2005). As noted previously, in the 1990s the World Bank and IMF (International Monetary Fund) began targeting poverty reduction in recipient countries. In the Highly Indebted Poor Countries initiative, debt relief was tied to the requirement of developing a Poverty Reduction Strategy Paper outlining the ways in which resources no longer tied to debt burden would be used towards reducing poverty. Another requirement was that the Poverty Reduction Strategy Paper be designed in a participatory way (Pellegrini, 2012).

Participatory governance practices also extend to decentralization processes. *Decentralization* entails devolving state functions to lower-level administrations. It can include the transfer of fiscal decisions, resources, and political authority, all of which is meant to promote local control in determining public policy (Long, 2001). The shift towards local institutions at the municipal level is viewed as being more accessible and "closer to the people," which presumably leads to poverty reduction and increasing equity (Gaventa, 2004). Decentralization is often accompanied by institutional reforms that open space for citizen engagement, which increases the political space for citizens to voice their opinions and hold governments accountable (Fung et al., 2003). Although not inherently reformative, the lack of radical change after two decades of decentralization around the world speaks to the limits of mainstream participatory efforts.

Transformative participation

A second broad category of participation can be conceptualized as *transformative*, given that its principle objective is to utilize participation as a way to dramatically transform the cultural, political, and/or economic structures that reproduce poverty and marginalization. Indeed, early proponents of participation, such as Brazilian educator Paulo Freire, sought to challenge "patterns of dominance" through empowerment (White, 2011). Waddington and Mohan (2004) equate empowerment with developing a personal political literacy, building consciousness and confidence to exercise agency. This personal development can initiate larger processes of bottom-up group mobilization around the collective experiences of marginalized groups that seek to challenge hegemonic order and market structures. Transformative participation often occurs in autonomous invented spaces of participation (Cornwall, 2003) to organize and undertake collective grassroots actions and tactics intended to resist existing structures (Miraftab, 2006). Transformative participation can also take place in invited spaces where larger structural shifts in state policy making can occur. Here, the act of participation is transformative if it implies a transfer of power.

While some critics have grown disillusioned with participation due to conflated understandings of the concept and ensuing problematic results (Cooke & Kothari, 2001), there has been a resurgence of the potential transformative possibility of participation through critical reflection (Cahill, 2007; Green, 2010; Kesby, 2005). Participation can contribute to lasting social change when it is not used as a quick fix or technical solution (Cornwall, 2003, p. 214). Locating participation in "radical politics of social transformation" reaffirms the concept's counter-hegemonic roots (Leal, 2007, p. 79). Hickey and Mohan (2005) propose the repositioning of participation within "radical politics of development" (p. 251) by reframing participation that merges facets of liberal citizenship, as in formal rights and political channels, with a civic republican approach based on citizens' collective engagement in decision-making. They outline the following conditions for transformative participation: 1) form part of a broader political and radical project; 2) move beyond the confines of particular interventions and participate in the "underlying process of development" towards social change (e.g. inviting citizens to engage with core state activities); and 3) secure citizenship participation in order to "progressively alter the processes of inclusion that operate within particular communities, and which govern the opportunities for individuals and groups to claim their rights to participation and resources."

The goal of transformative participation is to radically transform a situation to create meaningful social and economic change through empowerment by the participation of those excluded from economic or political processes. White (2011, p. 68) argues that "participation as *empowerment* is that the practical experience of being involved in considering options, making decisions, and taking collective action to fight injustice is itself transformative." The process of transformative participation seeks to exert control over decision-making, sharing knowledge and skills, and the redistribution of power, resources, and benefits (Saxena, 2011). While the goal is a structural transformation, the experience of reversing an injustice (or attempting to) is also viewed as meaningful and transformative in and of itself (White, 2011).

As it is typically understood as a movement "from below" to transform existing structures, the main actors of transformative participation are those making demands, the voice of the oppressed or dispossessed, citizens that are excluded from political and economic processes, who are often organized in community organizations and social movements. This includes people who organize, mobilize and make demands, and negotiate for greater participation at the decision-making level. Governments are also involved in civil society engagement through social reforms, the redistribution of wealth, and opening spaces for political participation. NGOs sometimes act as advocates for transformative participation and can be important allies in creating spaces for negotiating demands (White, 2011). Practices and examples of transformative participation include participatory action research, mobilization and social movements, and participatory governance, amongst others.

Participatory action research—The roots of this form of emancipatory participation are most often credited to Brazilian educator, Paulo Freire, who founded (in 1970) the school of participatory action research and its community-based research processes that sought to reverse injustices by transforming the structures that replicate poverty and marginalize the poorest. Influenced by Fanon's critique of imperialism and nationalism and his proposal of the redistribution of wealth, Freire's objective was to foster a system of education that valued students' experiences and local knowledge so that education would become a consciousness-raising tool for oppressed populations to "possess their own decision-making powers, free of oppressive and dehumanizing circumstances" (Leal, 2007, p. 71). This process of conscientization would act as a catalyst to advance political action and social transformation (Kindon et al., 2007; Kothari & Hickey, 2009).

Collective action—Participation existed before it was popularized in mainstream development projects, as people were building their own structures and forms of collective action. This type of participation is referred to as community collaboration or self-governance and can be understood as a form of collective decision-making, the "formation and application of social norms" that is exercised outside of institutionalized state mechanisms (Cielo, 2009, p. 11). This does not preclude collaboration with external institutions for resources or consultation (technical advice), but the decision-making control remains within the group (Pretty & Hine, 1999). Emphasis is placed on collaboration on a more level playing field, encouraging knowledge exchange and various contributions (Probst & Hagmann, 2003).

Mobilization/popular movements—The mobilization of dispossessed peoples refers to using several tactics that result in "real gains" with the goal of social transformation (Stiefel & Wolfe, 1994). It involves people taking action, united by a common cause (Saxena, 2011). A focus on issues, bringing together different people and motivations for a combined or coordinated effort, can sometimes eliminate or minimize class antagonisms. This can manifest itself as different groups fighting for their rights or interests using different tactics (e.g. collective bargaining). However, discord within social movements can arise, as creating solidarity amongst groups with varying interests can be difficult, particularly when it may mean foregoing group rights for the greater common good (Stiefel & Wolfe, 1994).

Participatory governance—This form of participatory governance differs from the one mentioned in the reformative category, as it seeks to deepen democratic governance through participation. The goal of strengthening participation is twofold: the inclusion of citizen voices to inform policies and improving accountability and responsiveness in institutions through institutional change (Gaventa, 2004, p. 27). Inclusive participation is driven by the notion that it creates a more active citizenship (participation as "right of citizenship"), with greater agency in the political arena (Lister, 1998, p. 288). Ackermann stresses the establishment of co-governance spaces, that is, inviting civil society into core state activities. This positive outcome can be observed in a number of examples around the world where participatory governance resulted in enhanced equity in local services (Osmani, 2000). Participatory budgeting in Porto Alegre, Brazil, is a well-cited case of increased public participation that challenged structural inequalities (Hickey & Mohan, 2005). Activists in Porto Alegre fought for greater public participation in deliberation over municipal budgets through inclusive budgetary decision-making. Once in power, the activist-supported political party *Partido dos Trabalhadores* (Workers' Party) implemented participatory budgeting (Mansuri & Rao, 2013). This process provided space for citizens, including marginalized groups, to make demands in hitherto exclusionary processes, thereby empowering citizens and improving the transparency and flow of information. Through participatory budgeting, improvements in people's lives based on expressed needs occurred through shifts in investments towards typically underfunded sectors of sanitation, health, housing, and education (Hickey & Mohan, 2005). Heller (2001) links the success of Porto Alegre's participatory budgeting to the social movement characteristics adopted by the political party that challenged structural inequalities. However, Mansuri and Rao (2013) note that the outcomes of participatory budgeting as it was introduced in other Brazilian cities varied substantially across municipalities, signalling the importance of local context and that alternative models of participation do not function in isolation from outside pressures.

Nominal participation

Worth noting is a third category of participation employed by various entities that cuts across ideologies. *Nominal participation* is a false type of participation insofar as it is typically used to legitimize a project or policy rather than seek genuine input or alternative ideas. Whereas advocates of reformative participation believe that certain participatory practices will lead to market improvements, nominal participation can be considered a "performance of participation"(Perreault, 2015), as the intent is to reinforce the standing social order. The intent of nominal participation is veiled by the haziness surrounding the concept and the prevalent notion that any form of participation should be cultivated. Essentially, nominal participation is a repurposing of the concept of participation or, as Brown (2004, p. 249) aptly states, "the co-optation of faddish language in the service of the status quo."

As with reformative participation, spaces of participation are tightly controlled invited spaces (Cornwall, 2002) that occur at official venues where agendas are carefully circumscribed by external agents in a way that curtails effective public engagement. Here, meaningful participation is not fostered, because questions and discussions are discouraged, resulting in a one-way flow of superficial information to citizens from officials or authorities; participation is promoted only in appearance. This kind of empty participation legitimates decisions taken by "power holders" because it appears as though all stakeholders' voices were considered (Arnstein, 1969). These meetings merely amount to "displays of participation" (White, 2011).

The intended outcome of nominal participation can be to reinforce the status quo of power dynamics, gain legitimacy, and appease parts of the population. Participation is used to depoliticize activities and enlist community members' support for specific projects and practices (McNeish, 2013). The bureaucratic mechanisms of nominal participation serve to reproduce social order, state authority, and industry practices, while social inequalities remain obscured. On the other hand, poorly operationalized participation or lack of capacity to foster participation of the reformative or transformative kind can also lead to nominal participation.

Different state actors across the ideological spectrum exploit participatory practices towards their own ends; often, to gain access to funding, participatory practices must be included. Main actors are political parties and state representatives at all levels, NGOs that fail to incorporate participatory practices properly, and public or private companies whose official participatory mechanisms are largely hollow. Practices include community development, consultation, and informing.

Community development—Historically, nominal participation has been a technique of rule that can be traced back to colonial indirect rule (Midgley, 1986). Through community development, participation was viewed as an obligation of citizenship, promulgated in order to keep in check the "claims on the centre" (Hickey & Mohan, 2005). Today, nominal participation takes place most commonly in the form of consultative processes. Mosse (2003) argues that participatory practices in community development projects are most often aligned with external concerns. The participatory framework does not help reflect community interests; rather, it serves to make communities adopt institutional interests as their own: "both participation and its *denial in practice* were necessary to the management of reputation and the marketing of success" (Mosse, 2003, p. 193; emphasis in the original). These incongruences led Cooke and Kothari (2001) to label participation as the "new tyranny" of development, arguing that participation works to depoliticize development; they seriously questioned whether the approach was worth saving. Even critics from within donor institutions questioned the validity of participation, decrying a lack of systematic analysis of the outcomes of participatory practices.

Consultation and informing—Oftentimes, institutionalized laws and mechanisms, such as the consultation process, are used towards nominal participation ends. The consultative participation method gathers views and information from people involved in or impacted by a project in an effort to help shape planning. Generally, the project's "problems and solutions" are defined by external professionals, who also determine who can access the consultation process (Brown, 2004; Pretty & Hine, 1999). As there is no obligation to incorporate views resulting from consultations, dominant stakeholders maintain control over crucial decisions (Probst & Hagmann, 2003), thereby rendering the consultative process merely an information session.

Reformative, transformative and nominal participation in Bolivia

Drawing on the foregoing framework, this section examines moments and spaces of participation in Bolivia in general and attempts to categorize them according to reformative, transformative, and nominal participation. Table 3.2 provides a summary of this analysis. As with any typology, realities on the ground never fit neatly into a conceptual framework. In practice, public participation in Bolivia flows across reformative, transformative, and nominal categories, often encompassing more than one at a time. It is useful to think of these forms of participation fitting into a spectrum. As such, rather than attempting to describe these practices in strict typological order, I have opted to explain them chronologically, identifying changes in intent and outcome over time and endeavouring to distil from these practices typological features that help us better understand the opportunities, constraints, and contradictions of public participation in Bolivia today. This requires an analysis of local norms of representation and decision-making and how these are negotiated and shifting (Cleaver, 2001). In the end, the transformative potential of MAS's intended participatory policies has been thwarted or subsumed by more reformative and nominal practices, creating a collage of outcomes with no clear future. Table 3.2 is, therefore, meant to serve as a heuristic guide to a very complicated situation.

Prominent examples of transformative participation practices in Bolivia can be traced back to the organized working class formed following the 1952 Revolution. For most of the twentieth century, the Bolivian Workers Confederation was the authority for the national workers movement (Dunkerley, 1984) and fought for recognition and levels of participation that could be classified as citizen power. The most powerful base of the Bolivian Workers Confederation was the Bolivian mine workers. Though they were a small percentage of the population, their importance lay in the fact that 25% of the country's GDP was related to mining (Dunkerley, 1984). During the 1950s, *controles obreros*, or worker control, gave mining workers veto power in decision-making in the management of nationalized mines (España et al., 2003). Through this worker co-management, the Mining Corporation of Bolivia sought to transform socio-economic conditions through changes in the mining judicial system, but ultimately failed due to the "appropriation, manipulation, and instrumentalization of [worker control] by the government and party politics" (Cielo, 2009, p. 8). In the 1980s, a type of worker co-management was practiced in public assemblies (Cajias, 2009). The authority of these groups declined as their power weakened in the neoliberal era after the collapse of the mining sector due to falling tin

Table 3.2 Summary of reformative, transformative, and nominal participation in Bolivia

Type of participation	Conceptualization	Intended outcome	Actors in Bolivia	Tools and practices
Reformative	State mandated institution-building of participatory practices to extend "marketization of land and natural resources" (extension of neoliberalism); devolving decision-making to the local level, "closer to the people," to diminish centralized government; legal recognition of citizens' (civil society) right to exert control over public institutions in a prescribed manner; dependent on state funding/resources; based on "pro-poor" policies.	Integrate citizens into defined spaces of participation that would facilitate economic restructuring; improve planning outcomes and governmental efficiency (i.e. reduce corruption); bring autonomous local organizations into the institutional fold.	International financial institutions (World Bank); political parties (ADN, MNR); international cooperation and NGOs; Catholic Church; vigilance committees; "primary stakeholders" (targeted populations, Grassroots Territorial Organizations)	Policies and institutional reforms (Bolivian Poverty Reduction Strategy); Law of Popular Participation (LPP); decentralization, National Dialogue Mechanism of Social Control; development interventions
Transformative	Creating spaces for political participation in decision-making for hitherto excluded groups	Achieve an equitable system that corresponds to people's needs by establishing popular policies.	Social organizations, unions, and networks (*Coordinadora*, COB, CSUTCB, NGOs);	Co-governance (*poder dual*); popular mobilizations, marches; community

	(particularly marginalized, Indigenous, and local organizations; women) to destabilize the (neoliberal) regime.	mechanisms for participation; particular attention to Bolivians' control over natural resources (i.e. making them public).	community groups and neighbourhood associations (Grassroots Territorial Organizations, *juntas vecinales*, FEJUVE); political parties (MAS)	collaboration (autonomous self-management, communitarian assemblies); Constitution (2009)
Nominal	Hollow participation; poor administration of participatory mechanisms and/or instrumental use to quell opposition; paternalistic attitude towards more inclusive governance.	Ensure entrenched interests remain intact; manage competing demands.	Occurs at different spaces (national to local level) across ideological lines; political parties (MNR, MAS)	Institutionalized laws and mechanisms (LPP, Constitution); consultations (*Consulta previa*); elite capture

prices in the 1980s. The influence of these militant miners can nevertheless still be felt throughout the country, as they migrated to the Chapare region and peri-urban centres, passing on these lessons (Crespo et al., 2004).

After 40 years of military-authoritarian regimes, democratic elections were held in 1985, though voter turnout was low. At the time, Bolivia was deemed the poorest and most indebted country in South America. A neoliberal economic order was established soon after the 1985 elections. What can be categorized as reformative participation was introduced through World Bank sanctioned "pro-poor" policies, viewed as the institution-building accompaniment to economic restructuring. These second-generation reforms were intended to ease the harsh macroeconomic restructuring initiated a decade earlier (Pellegrini, 2012), the logic being that improvement in economic growth would follow from increasing the population's participation in the market, as integrating citizens into defined spaces of participation would hold local governments accountable. The focus was to simultaneously reduce central government spending and improve local government efficiency, that is, to reduce corruption by increasing accountability to local populations. The intended beneficiaries of this reformative participation were the poorest sectors of Bolivia's population. Tools and practices were put in place to increase the participation of previously excluded groups, including Indigenous people and women, typically comprised of "add-and-stir" technical solutions, with little attention paid to local context. Paradoxically, these targeted groups were the most marginalized by overarching economic reforms. Contrary to the intended outcome, the strategies and mechanisms employed occasioned limited participation, and the economic reforms created a wider gulf between rich and poor in Bolivia that led to further political instability (Postero, 2017, 2010).

The political parties in power during the neoliberal era that implemented participation policies include the Revolutionary National Movement (MNR) under the administration of Gonzalo (Goni) Sánchez de Lozada (1993–7; 2002–3), and the National Democratic Action (ADN) under Hugo Banzer (1997–2001), Jorge Quiroga (2001–2), and Carlos Mesa administrations (2003–5). Support for these participatory reforms came from the Catholic Church, viewed as one of the main actors in civil society (Aguilar Miranda & Miranda Hernández, 2012). Many externally funded NGOs working in Bolivia aligned their development projects with international participation priorities (that adhered to reformative intent).[1]

The Law of Popular Participation (LPP) is the key piece of legislation that first recognized civil society's right to exert control over public institutions. It also demonstrates how the same tool of participation can be utilized to different ends: first as a legislative mechanism to implement reformative participation that, in turn, inspired the struggle for more inclusive participation.

The LPP was a state-led initiative introduced in 1994 that officially recognized Bolivia as a plurinational state, acknowledging the various existing nationalities and territories within Bolivia. It aimed to amplify spaces of participation, meeting long-standing demands of historically excluded sectors of the population, notably Indigenous groups and women (Hippert, 2011). In the LPP, social control is conceived of as practices to ensure accountability and transparency in local government, the right and responsibility to supervise and evaluate results and impacts of public policies and participatory processes of decision-making. España et al. (2003) thereby argue that this set of authorized techniques and practices shape social control into a state instrument.

At the municipal level, so-called vigilance committees (*comités de vigilancia* in Spanish) were put in place to carry out social control: to monitor municipal budgets and spending, ensure co-participation resources are properly administered, and ensure all funds are accounted for (Ayo, 2004). A study by Urioste and Baldomar (1996) identified a major problem with the technical competencies (e.g. technical knowledge to elaborate a budget) required from members of the vigilance committees (Cielo, 2009). These technical requirements make it difficult to elect qualified members from a typical community, thereby limiting or inhibiting the exercise of social control (Cunill Grau, 2000). Cielo (2009, p. 8) argues that this exclusionary quality of the vigilance committees relates back to the issue of limiting development to technical solutions that are only within the grasp of certain experts, "positioned as agents with capacity to diagnose deficiencies in others."

Together with the accompanying Law of Administrative Decentralization and Law of Municipalities, the LPP initiated the decentralization process in Bolivia. A global trend in the 1990s, decentralization programs were favoured internationally as a remedy to assumed inefficiency and corruption in centralized governments (WB, 1997). The outcome was the creation of 311 municipal districts in Bolivia (today's total is 339), overwhelmingly in rural areas where municipal administrations did not previously exist (INE, 2014; Kohl, 2003).

Through decentralization, decision-making powers and the distribution of state funds devolved to the municipal level. To better respond to local needs, underrepresented *campesino*[2] and neighbourhood organizations, now legally recognized as Grassroots Territorial Organizations, or OTBs in their Spanish acronym, were included in the institutionalized participatory process. Yearly, the OTBs submit proposals to compete for municipal development funding, a system that is still in place today. The goal of lowering central government expenditures was achieved by shifting the responsibility for the funding and execution of these programs to municipalities. However, municipalities often lack the capabilities to fulfil demands in infrastructure and services (Kohl, 2003). For this reason, the decentralization process did not prove to be an easy or successful transition to governmental efficiency. Of the low rate of community proposals that were completed and approved, few consisted of truly participatory citizen efforts; rather they were elaborated in mayors' offices, where problems of financial mismanagement and corruption abound (Kohl, 2003). In areas of robust community organizing that could benefit from the LPP instruments, there were insufficient economic resources to support the initiatives (Kohl, 2003).

Hesketh and Morton (2014) point out that the LPP increased spaces of decision-making at the local level, yet questions of resource management and the associated economic power no longer formed part of these decisions. Kohl (2003) suggests the LPP served to reorient people's focus towards local processes, namely competition for limited local resources, and away from resistance to economic restructuring at the national level. Established organizations such as the Bolivian Workers Confederation and the Bolivian Unitary Syndical Peasant Workers Confederation (CSUTCB) that historically acted as a counterweights to state powers and mediators between society and state were now fractured due to the heightened localism provoked by the establishment of OTBs (Regalsky, 2010). OTBs now superseded other groups legally and split territories and, in turn, the base membership of pre-existing unions (Regalsky & Laurie, 2007). More damningly, the strength of workers unions diminished once collective agreements and negotiations disintegrated under the privatization process, finally to be eliminated as representative bodies in the Law of Political Parties. The latter stipulated popular representation to be exercised through political parties and their alliances (Carazas et al., 2009). So, while the LPP (Law of Popular Participation) succeeded in bringing autonomous local organizations into the institutional fold through the creation of OTBs, it was done at the expense and weakening of established organizations. While the LPP legally recognized local organizations, it did not change the power dynamics of local decision-making practices. The city councils remain under the control of political parties, where the local elite's power is reinforced (Postero, 2010).

Though problematic as a tool of reformative participation, the LPP is also viewed as a catalyst for more transformative opportunities, as Bolivians used the new law as a basis to demand rights. In fact, it is distrust and dissatisfaction with the LPP that led social movement organizations to resist and question these legal mechanisms. Komadina (2009) views this challenge to power as an important non-institutionalized form of social control. Similarly, Cortéz (2007, p. 115) sees social control moving towards "a tool of confrontation and de-legitimization of the State." The same participatory mechanisms that promoted neoliberal reforms became the basis for making claims for more transformative participatory governance. The LPP is still in place today, and the OTBs created under this law have strengthened and increased in number since the law's inception.

At best, reformative participation can improve an existing situation by changing expectations of public participation. Good governance agendas can inadvertently give rise to popular movements and "spaces of citizenship" (Corbridge et al., 2005). In the same vein, Masaki (2004, p. 126) posits that, "tyrannical aspects of peoples' participation can also be accompanied by transformative forces." Williams (2004, p. 240) also argues that, "any configuration of power/knowledge opens up its own particular spaces and moments for resistance." In Bolivia, a fundamental questioning of representative democracy and the party system resulted in the re-emergence of proposals and demands for a constituent assembly, referendum, and constitutional changes.

The demand for a constituent assembly to be institutionalized in the Constitution can be traced back to several Indigenous marches on La Paz, the seat of government at the Presidential Palace, throughout the 1990s (Aguilar Miranda & Miranda Hernández, 2012). These marches are credited with popularizing the debates surrounding the demands for a constituent assembly that had not previously formed part of discussions outside political or academic realms (Aguilar Miranda & Miranda Hernández, 2012, p. 30). The marches in the early 1990s helped spur the ratification of the Indigenous and Tribal Peoples Convention 169 of the International Labour Organization that led up to the constitutional reforms of 1994 recognizing the multi-ethnic and pluri-cultural makeup of the country and the recognition of Indigenous peoples rights in Article 1 and Article 171 of the 1994 Constitution (Aguilar Miranda & Miranda Hernández, 2012, p. 28). In Bolivia, systemic racism endures against the majority Indigenous population that has historically been excluded from participation in a state controlled by white or *mestizo*[3] elites. For this reason, opening spaces for political participation in decision-making via increased opportunities for Indigenous and local organizations is paramount.

The National Dialogue was one such initiative to bolster public participation by the Banzer administration in 1997.[4] As part of the Bolivian Poverty Reduction Strategy, the National Dialogue was organized as an official public consultation to flesh out policy lines and priorities for poverty reduction (Aguilar Miranda & Miranda Hernández, 2012). The initiative was also an attempt to reduce tensions and improve waning government legitimacy, evidenced by the numerous protests in Bolivia due to rising dissatisfaction with the participatory process and the weight of structural reforms (Cielo, 2009). At the time, Banzer stated that the National Dialogue was the "best form of citizen participation in the strengthening of democracy" (Aguilar Miranda & Miranda Hernández, 2012, p. 12). However, the National

Dialogue did not enjoy broad or diverse participation from rural and urban workers' unions, whereas the Catholic Church was allocated considerable influence in these discussions (Pellegrini, 2012). Because people were excluded from the process, the reforms did little to provoke real change and consolidated the formal structures of the existing liberal democracy. As a result, these efforts did not meet the demands of the poorer Bolivian sectors that continued to mobilize in the streets. The Bolivian Workers Confederation was particularly vocal in its rejection of the National Dialogue, as political parties were not meeting demands for increased participation.

In response to protestors who demanded modification of the Constitution to strengthen participatory democracy and put an end to the monopoly of political parties, a second National Dialogue was organized in 2000 (Aguilar Miranda & Miranda Hernández, 2012). The result of this process was a Law of National Dialogue that introduced qualitative consultation methods for social control nationally and at the departmental level in the form of referendums, popular consultations, and direct elections of officials with the mediation of parties. The main political parties (MNR, ADN, MIR) were fairly opposed to any changes to the party system, fearing it would lead to instability and destroy representational democracy (Zegada et al., 2011; Cielo, 2009). Nonetheless, constitutional reforms for public participation were incorporated in an Agenda of Reforms presented by Banzer in February 2001. In the same year, a proposal by the so-called Council of Citizens was put forth for constitutional reform that avoided the possibility of a constituent assembly and did not include mechanisms for participatory reforms. Social organizations deemed this council illegitimate and viewed their proposal as another imposition "from above." For Banzer, the purpose of the National Dialogue was to articulate and have approved the policies of the Bolivian Poverty Reduction Strategy as required for debt forgiveness. This goal was ultimately achieved with some difficulty (Pellegrini, 2012).

This type of participation constitutes a top-down approach, as institutions and organizations identified groups to include in the process that did not deviate from donors' rules and requirements. Indeed, the "targeted poor" to be included in invited spaces of the National Dialogue and legally recognized under law excluded established grassroots organizations. The actors responsible for implementing this kind of reformative participation in Bolivia were vested in promoting participation for the purpose of guaranteeing debt forgiveness. Due to the conceptual limitations of this participation, namely, that its intended goal did not change structures that marginalize certain groups, the main outcome was to maintain the status quo of those in power rather than effect change (Cornwall & Brock, 2005). Eventually, the mechanism for social control established under the National Dialogue was deemed unsuccessful due to mishandled funds (Pellegrini, 2012).

Failure to open decision-making spaces combined with economic restructuring that further impoverished the country, again sparked outrage and protest. Left and Indigenous social movements were at the forefront of mobilizations making demands for transformative participation at the height of activism from 2000 to 2005 (Hesketh & Morton, 2014). Anti-government coalitions formed between Indigenous movements, neighbourhood and community associations (such as *juntas vecinales*, FEJUVE—*Federación de juntas vecinales*), and labour movements and agrarians unions (including the CSUTCB) brought together by coordinating bodies presented an unrelenting opposition to neoliberal policies, which led to the collapse of Sánchez de Lozada's administration with his resignation in 2003 (Kohl & Farthing, 2006; Lazar, 2007).

The resource wars of that period (Water Wars of 2000 and 2003 and Gas War of 2003) were pivotal moments that called for greater participation in decision-making processes, particularly in the realm of resource management. These resource wars came to symbolize the lack of agency that people felt and the need for greater accountability. The intended outcome of transformative participation is to transform social relations to achieve a more equitable system that meets people's needs. In Bolivia, this goal was most visibly tied to the fight against privatization and for control over the country's natural resource management. Part of the struggle to reverse privatization was a redistribution of power, the demand for influence over policy and politics that had long been in the hands of a few that did not work in citizens' interests.

La Coordinadora, a coordinating body formed during the Water War, supported and spread the idea of forming a constituent assembly as a popular mechanism to define state policy (Torrico et al., 2013). Through the medium of radio and posters, they publicized a document in 2002 titled, "For a different country, with participation of the people, let's build a democracy from below," proposing the constituent assembly be legalized in the Constitution (Aguilar Miranda & Miranda Hernández, 2012, p. 30). It suggested that the composition of the assembly be as follows: half of the members to be territorial representatives, and the other half to be sector representatives (workers, Indigenous business leaders, *campesinos*), with Indigenous–*campesinos* reaching a total of 128 members of the assembly. This proposal intended to reconcile the strong social demands for a popular assembly and the constituent assembly.

Finally, in 2004, the constituent assembly was institutionalized; this was viewed as a triumph of social sectors that wished to widen democracy (Aguilar Miranda & Miranda Hernández, 2012, p. 26). In November 2004, the Law of Constitutional Reform was approved that incorporated the realization of a constituent assembly, elaborating and approving the Law to Call the Constituent Assembly, the election of assembly members, and the sanction of a new Constitution (Aguilar Miranda & Miranda Hernández, 2012, p. 26). However, the constituent assembly as a "new beginning" was undermined and viewed as more of a technicality by some in government. Indeed, the new Constitution would not be established until the MAS (Movement Towards Socialism—*Movimiento Al Socialismo*) government assumed office in 2006.

The MAS party, led by Evo Morales, leader of the *cocalero* (coca farmers) movement, presented itself as the "party of social movements," thus breaking away from the traditional party structure. With widespread support, MAS ran on a platform of *proceso de cambio* (process of change) that promised a shift away from neoliberalism and (neo)colonialism. Morales was propelled into office in 2005 with an absolute majority of the vote for the first time in Bolivia's democratic period (Dangl, 2019). The change in government signalled a shift towards transformative participation, where social control can include invited spaces of institutional practices and also invented spaces (Cornwall, 2002) of deliberation where decisions, agreements, and accords are made from below. Formal/state spaces, which in the reformative participation category are spaces with pre-determined outcomes, can also be transformative if the state is genuinely interested in inviting people to the table with the aim of radical transformation. With the new MAS government, social control was understood as an important instrument for society. Raúl Prada, ex-constituent member of MAS, expressed that social control is the greatest affirmation of participatory democracy: "it is a new relationship between state and society, a relation where society takes the initiative, and the state is converted to a tool of society" (as quoted in "Según el oficialismo", 2009).

The Right to Social Control as a tool of direct participation appears in Articles 241 and 242 of the new (2009) Constitution. The text stipulates that civil society has social control over public management at all state levels, over public companies and institutions (including mixed private-public), and the quality of public services. For example, the new Constitution includes forms of direct participation by collective and individual subjects that can not only legitimize or delegitimize the constituted political power but also can regulate and form the institutionalism of the plurinational state. Paragraph 5 of Article 241 stipulates that civil society has the right to provide input on definitions of the structure of participation. The forms, structure, and composition of social control and participation are meant to emerge from agreements with different organizations at all levels, taking into account various interests in civil society (Medina Hoyos, 2009). Article 7 of the new Constitution establishes the constitutional basis for people to exercise social control, through representation or directly. Article

26 recognizes the right of citizens to direct collective or individual participation in public matters. The Right to Petition (Article 24) and the Right to Access to Information (Article 21 No. 6) related to participation and social control are also present in the new Constitution. Further, the Authority of Audit and Social Control, dependent on corresponding ministries, replaced the former regulatory entities, "superintendents," from the Sánchez de Lozada administration. Replacing the superintendents was meant to signal a break with neoliberal policies and practices of reformative participation from that era.

The complicated process of how the new Constitution was finalized sheds light on the contested nature of social control and participation and the different conceptualizations thereof. The MAS regime ushered in principles of social control, now recognized as a new democratic mechanism of the plurinational state. Before reaching this point, however, the approach of institutionalizing social control went through various iterations. Initially, a plurinational social power was proposed in a Unity Pact at the Constituent Assembly. This social power was proposed as a separate branch of the state, independent and autonomous from other powers (Article 114, *Pacto de Unidad*). The proposal was heavily debated and caused a rift within MAS between the proponents of social power that viewed it as an alternative to representative democracy and the factions that viewed the proposal as unviable. This tension is indicative of the struggles faced by MAS throughout their governance; that is, the balance between staying in power and staying dedicated to their base. At its core, the disagreement was about upholding the party system versus finding an alternative way that would incorporate genuine transformative participation.

Finally, the text of the new Constitution was approved with no mention of an institution of social control of equal hierarchy to other state powers. Rather, social control was defined as follows: "the sovereign people, through civil society, will participate in decision-making of public policies" (EPB, 2009). However, even this aspect of decision-making was ultimately dropped in the final edit of the new Constitution in order to avoid potential conflicts with the executive branches of government. As such, it limits the transformative potential of participation, arguably reinforcing the status quo, as the "liberal capitalist state is not threatened at its core" (Webber, 2010, np).

MAS representatives later stated that a separate social control branch of government was decided against so that civil society participants would maintain a critical distance and not become civil servants and part of the state ('Según el oficialismo', 2009). Komadina (2009) characterizes this as the limits of the "process of change" and the difficulty of imagining a real alternative democracy, one of the flaws of a liberal representative system. He argues that civil society forms part of a democratic citizen tradition that has legitimacy through indirect power in civil society. The end goal is not to exercise power but to provide a system of control of civil servants and elected representatives. Social control as it is in the new Constitution, according to Komadina, can help to deepen democracy but it can also be subject to political instrumentalization.

This political instrumentalization of social control has occurred to an extent in Bolivia. MAS has been criticized for not delivering on their proposed changes and has been reproached for absorbing leaders of social movements, forming clientelistic relations with their base, placating opposition, and disregarding certain marginalized groups (Interview, Regalsky, 2014). A strong rhetoric of participation exists, but participatory practices and social control are not supported by concrete, sustainable, or meaningful undertakings. For example, OTBs can make decisions on a community level, but their influence beyond these official points of engagement is limited.

Part of the problem is that the language in the new Constitution provides sweeping generalizations about social control for Bolivian citizens, but there is little in the way of concrete protocol around practices. One of the reasons for being vague was that some Bolivians feared the greater role attributed to social movements and framed social control as a "capture of the state" ("Según el oficialismo," 2009), worrying that too much power given to social movements would create conflict within the legal and administrative systems. Others were concerned that practices of community justice, such as public lynching, would emerge as common and acceptable and that social control would lead to criminal groups taking over the government (Sánchez, 2008).

These fears overestimated the power of social control in municipalities as overseen by OTBs, who are limited to inspecting authorities and their budgets. State entities, including institutions that manage public resources such as Semapa, have the onus to facilitate spaces of participation and social control by civil society (Moreno, 2009). In this area, there seems to be little guidance as to the particularities of what public participation might look like, with different interpretations and definitions of social control confusing the protocol. Rather than a takeover of government, as speculated by some, it appears the opposite has been true. There is evidence that the implementation of official social control has resulted in the co-optation of social movements, with many having been absorbed into government.

MAS's position as the "party of social movements" has translated into the placement of social movement leaders in official party positions and the recognition of social movements, especially certain Indigenous movements but not into granting much access to the Ministries (Stefanoni, 2007). This means many social movements no longer have their leaders, who are now in intermediate government positions, while at the same time subordinated to higher state levels of administration. Regalsky (2010) argues this has the combined effect of fragmenting movements and reinforcing the state's power and legitimacy. The vigilance committees established under the LPP, now often referred to as social control committees, also remain subjected to networks of clientelism linked to municipal authorities (Carazas et al., 2009; Moreno, 2009). Once a political instrument for change, MAS lost many of its transformative characteristics when it became a political party (Hesketh & Morton, 2014). It shifted its strategy from a transformative participatory framework back to traditional electoral politics, resulting in a less radical version of social movement demands and proposals (Hesketh & Morton, 2014). What began as a transformative process turned into the defence of the nation state and the very same institutions that were so heavily questioned during the resource wars (Regalsky, 2010). One of the goals of transformative participation in Bolivia was to put an end to the monopoly of political parties, but this did not happen. Rather, it replaced one regime with another, and social movements were de-radicalized as they were absorbed by the state.

The Law of Public Participation and the Poverty Reduction Strategy Paper are still in use today. In fact, the National Development Plan, developed to complement the Poverty Reduction Strategy, represents a substantial part of Morales' development objectives (Pellegrini, 2012). While some of the social movements' requests were included in the National Development Plan, they were not formally involved in its design process, while many of the previous reformative neoliberal processes continue to be employed. Indeed, many actions taken by Evo Morales and MAS have led scholars to question whether his government has been as "post-neoliberal" as they claim. Webber (Webber, 2011, p. 170) characterizes Morales' continued support or assistance to global capital as "reconstituted neoliberalism," an extension of neoliberalism with the addition of Indigenous rights.

An illustration of this paradox lies within MAS's rhetoric of respecting *Pachamama* (Mother Earth) and actions that extend resource extraction, which contradict the former commitment to environmental protection (Postero, 2010; Hippert, 2011). Decision-making in this area has not devolved to the general public. The existing consultation process undertaken by public and private institutions in the resource extraction sector does not take seriously or incorporate the ideas or concerns of "primary stakeholders" but merely informs them of pre-determined actions. In effect, the "voice" of populations and groups affected by resource extraction are not included in decision-making, making participatory practices in this sector largely nominal (Perreault, 2015).[5]

Reformative participatory mechanisms have allowed MAS to absorb local leadership and fragment movements by appointing social movement leaders into low- to middle-level administrative positions and entering into clientelistic relations. Dissenting voices also calmed once participation and social control were institutionalized in the new Constitution, despite the lack of clarity on its implementation and practical functioning. Poor implementation of transformative participatory practices due to little guidance is compounded by the problem of limited administrative capacity (Kohl & Farthing, 2012). Heller (2001) contends that certain conditions encourage participation: a competent central state, a strong civil society, and a well-organized political impetus such as a political party that adopts social movement qualities. Often, however, such ideal conditions are not in place, and limiting factors or conditions can stunt transformation. In these cases, participation with a transformative intent can lead to improvements but also encounter obstacles by which it devolves into nominal participation. It is also possible that no manipulative or malicious intent exists. Civil servants may simply lack the capacity or commitment to foster spaces of participation and instead adopt a passive attitude to participation that does not in fact take into account the public's demands (Pretty, 2008). This can be observed in Bolivian institutions that purport to practice social control but often devolve into a mechanical practice of "ticking boxes."

Transformative participation is present and more tangible locally, however, notably amongst community groups and social movements, and the influence of these communitarian participatory practices must not be overlooked. The robust forms of participation stemming from *ayllus*, Indigenous communities more isolated in the northern plains of the Andes, are founded on self-government principles of solidarity and reciprocity (Larson, 1988). These practices inform social organization actors and significantly influence Indigenous mobilization. Autonomous forms of community government also exist in neighbourhoods that do not necessarily identify as Indigenous but where self-government and collective organization was necessary due to uneven development and lack of state provision of basic needs, such as education, health, and housing, ultimately rousing demands for autonomy (Harten, 2011; Zegada et al., 2011). Because state institutions in Bolivia have been historically weak or absent, there is a mistrust of the state and the view that they do not act in people's interests. That is why, despite the broad support that MAS has enjoyed, protecting the right to social auto-determination has become important because people want to "decide horizontally and autonomously about their own needs" without government intervention (Olivera, 2014, p. 64).

However, as Cielo (2009, p. 10) points out, inequalities can exist in the public sphere and civil society. She underlines Edgardo Lander's argument on how some literature on civil society paints the "state as authoritative, inefficient, corrupt, clientelistic, while civil society is always seen as the bearer of creativity, efficiency, liberty." The popularity of participation in recent years has led to a valorization of local knowledge and practices. Advocates of a commons property model of collective ownership tend to romanticize communities (Mehta, 2001). Yet the idealization of "community" can serve to minimize or ignore existing local coercive structures, detracting from broader relations of power that contribute to local problems (Fine, 1999; Mohan & Stokke, 2000; Williams, 2004). As Bakker (2007, p. 246) notes, the "commons can be exclusive and regressive, as well as inclusive and progressive." Participation is not always inclusive when decision-making power and resources are not devolved to the whole community and advantage local elites, replacing dominant power with others. Participation is also prone to elite capture as local elites can influence decisions in their favour, sometimes creating barriers for those with fewer resources, leading to an exacerbation of unequal circumstances. In this sense participation does not necessarily work towards balancing "power relations between and among social groups" (Hippert, 2011, p. 499).

Participation also becomes nominal when participatory mechanisms and public opinion are rejected, as evidenced by the conditions that led to the 2019 national electoral crisis and subsequent installation of a repressive interim government headed by Jeanine Áñez.[6] Controversy surrounded Evo Morales' campaign for re-election, as he was intent to run again despite having reached the constitutional term limit. The referendum held in 2016 to extend the number of terms one can serve as President was voted down by a slight majority—a sign of people's changing attitudes towards MAS. However, the party pushed back against the outcome and the Constitutional Court annulled the referendum results in 2017, allowing Morales to run for a fourth consecutive term. A party using participatory mechanisms to try to reach a political goal and then dismissing those same mechanisms when the outcome is not in their favour is a consummate example of nominal participation. The "*voto no*" (I voted no) campaign, headed by a faction of Bolivians intent on halting Morales' re-election, turned into weeks of protest following MAS's alleged fraud on election night in November 2019. This political crisis led to Morales' departure from office and exile and Áñez's self-appointment as interim President with the support of military and conservative politicians. Her right-wing government enacted violent suppression of protests, gravely mismanaged the pandemic response, and politicized Covid-19 to sanction police brutality and postpone re-elections three times. The turbulent year of government came to a close in November 2021, when the MAS party won a majority vote under new leadership. However, recent anti-MAS protests by coca growers from the Yungas region demonstrate that political instability in Bolivia has not ended. In terms of participation, at the national level, it has remained largely nominal. Social control and participation have been relegated to acceptable realms at certain scales, as long as these initiatives do not pose a direct threat to positions of power.

Conclusion

The typology of reformative, transformative, and nominal participation laid out in this chapter serves as a heuristic reference point for deciphering different types of participation in Bolivia. The realities on the ground are such that participatory practices in the country do not fit neatly into these categories, but the framework nevertheless helps to shed light on different understandings of participation and the tensions created by them. Although there appears to be a broad consensus that participation is important, particularly within public institutions, the lack of clarity surrounding the meaning of participation and the inherent tensions between different perspectives contribute to confusion as to what participation should be.

The main conclusions to be drawn from this analysis are that 1) all three types of participation exist to varying degrees in Bolivia, and 2) that the outcomes of participatory practices can vary greatly from their intent. Most importantly, the promise of transformative participation under the MAS government has not been fulfilled by state institutions, and, as a result, current practices of social control in the country are largely nominal.

Notes

1 Reformative participation was sustained by NGOs that promoted development in line with economic development goals such as micro-credit schemes to bring people into the market fold.

2 *Campesino* is the term denoting people residing in the countryside who may identify as Indigenous culturally or linguistically.

3 *Mestizo* is a category referring to someone of mixed Indigenous and non-Indigenous decent. However, it is an ambiguous and loaded term tied to historical racist assimilationist policies in Bolivia and across Latin America (Canessa, 2004; Rivera Cusicanqui, 2010).

4 Another initiative was the *Foro Jubileo* in 2000, hosted by the Catholic Church, where a national proposal for a social control mechanism was debated, although to little consequence.

5 In 2010, Morales hosted an international congress on the Rights of Mother Earth in Tiquipaya, Bolivia, as a counter to the Copenhagen Accord. The congress concluded with the penning of a Universal Declaration on Mother Earth Rights submitted by the Bolivian government to the United Nations. However, the constructive aspects of the congress were offset by a notable lack of attention to Bolivian development plans. To highlight this omission, an unofficial working group (*Mesa 18*) was organized after being banned from the official agenda. The workshop discussed mining, oil, and gas exploration plans, such as the Trans-Oceanic Highway (TIPNIS) projects that organizers argued lead to environmental degradation and displacement of Indigenous communities (Fieldwork observation, 2011).

6 For a comprehensive account of these events see Becker and Farthing (2021): *Coup: A story of violence and resistance in Bolivia.*

References

Ackerman, J. (2004). Co-governance for accountability: Beyond "exit" and "voice". *World Development*, *32*(3), 447–463. https://doi.org/10.1016/j.worlddev.2003.06.015

Aguilar Miranda, L. A., & Miranda Hernández, M. A. (2012). La participación política: Entre la concesión institucional y la conquista popular. In M. A. Gandarillas (Ed.), *Democracia participativa: ¿Realidad o espejismo?* (pp. 7–33). CEDIB.

Arnstein, S. R. (1969). A ladder of citizen participation. *Journal of the American Institute of Planners*, *35*(4), 216–224. https://doi.org/10.1080/01944366908977225

Ayo, D. (2004). *El control social en Bolivia: Una reflexión sobre el comité de vigilancia, el mecanismo de control social y demás formas de control social.* Grupo Nacional de Trabajo por la Participación.

Bakker, K. (2007). The "commons" versus the "commodity": Alter-globalization, anti-privatization and the human right to water in the Global South. *Antipode*, *39*, 430–455.

Becker, T., & Farthing, L. (2021). *Coup: A story of violence and resistance in Bolivia.* Haymarket Books.

Brown, D. (2004). Participation in poverty reduction strategies: Democracy strengthened or democracy undermined? In S. Hickey & G. Mohan (Eds.), *Participation: From tyranny to transformation?: Exploring new approaches to participation in development* (pp. 237–250). ZED Books; Distributed exclusively in the U.S. by Palgrave Macmillan.

Cahill, C. (2007). The personal is political: Developing new subjectivities through participatory action research. *Gender, Place & Culture*, *14*(3), 267–292. https://doi.org/10.1080/09663690701324904

Cajias, L. (2009). Del control social a la captura del estado. *Los Tiempos*.

Canessa, A. (2004). Reproducing racism: Schooling and race in highland Bolivia. *Race Ethnicity and Education*, *7*, 185–204.

Carazas, M., Icuña, S., & Apaza, N. (2009). Participación popular y control social: Exclusión y marginación de organizaciones sociales en la toma de desiciones sobre políticas públicas. *Villa Libre Cuadernos de Estudios Sociales Urbanos*, *4*, 139–153.

Cernea, M. M. (1991). *Putting people first: Sociological variables in rural development* (World Bank, Ed.; 2nd Rev. ed.). World Banks.

Chambers, R. (1994). The origins and practice of participatory rural appraisal. *World Development*, *22*(7), 953–969. https://doi.org/10.1016/0305-750X(94)90141-4

Chambers, R. (2011). Managing local participation: Rhetoric and reality. In A. Cornwall (Ed.), *The participation reader*. ZED Books.

Cielo, C. (2009). Aprendizajes desde el periurbano boliviano. *Villa Libre Cuadernos de Estudios Sociales Urbanos*, *4*, 7–35.

Cleaver, F. (2001). Institutions, agency, and the limitation of participatory approaches to development. In B. Cooke & U. Kothari (Eds.), *Participation: The new tyranny?* Zed Books.

Cohen, J. M., & Uphoff, N. T. (1980). Participation's place in rural development: Seeking clarity through specificity. *World Development*, *8*(3), 213–235. https://doi.org/10.1016/0305-750X(80)90011-X

Cooke, B., & Kothari, U. (Eds.). (2001). *Participation: The new tyranny?* Zed Books.

Corbridge, S., Williams, G., Srivastava, M., & Véron, R. (2005). *Seeing the state: Governance and governmentality in rural India*. Cambridge University Press.

Cornwall, A. (1998). Gender participation and the politics of difference. In I. Guijt & M. Kaul Shah (Eds.), *The myth of community: Gender issues in participatory development*. Intermediate Technology Publications.

Cornwall, A. (2002). *Making spaces, changing places: Situating participation in development*. IDS Working Paper, Institute of Development Studies.

Cornwall, A. (2003). Whose voices? Whose choices? Reflections on gender and participatory development. *World Development*, *31*(8), 1325–1342. https://doi.org/10.1016/S0305-750X(03)00086-X

Cornwall, A., & Brock, K. (2005). What do buzzwords do for development policy? A critical look at "participation", "empowerment" and "poverty reduction". *Third World Quarterly*, *26*(7), 1043–1060. https://doi.org/10.1080/01436590500235603

Cortéz, R. (2007). Control social. In *Contrapuntos al debate constituyente*. Plural.

Crawley, H. (1998). Living up to the empowerment claim? The potential of PRA. In I. Guijt & M. Kaul Shah (Eds.), *The myth of community: Gender issues in participatory development*. IIED.

Crespo, C., Peredo, C., & Omar, F. (2004). *Los regantes de Cochabamba en la guerra del agua: Presión social y negociación*. CESU-UMSS.

Cunill Grau, N. (2000). Responsabilización por el control social. In *Consejo Científico del CLAD: Responsabilización en la Nueva Gestión Pública Latinoamericana*. CLAD-BID-Editorial Universitaria de Buenos Aires.

Dangl, B. (2019). *The five hundred year rebellion: Indigenous movements and the decolonizaton of history in Bolivia*. AK Press.

Dunkerley, J. (1984). *Rebellion in the veins: Political struggle in Bolivia, 1952–82*. Verso.

España, R., Rozo, P., España, J. L., & Peres, J. A. (2003). *El control social en Bolivia: Un aporte a la reflexión y discusión*. Plural.

Estado Plurinacional de Bolivia (EPB). (2009). *Nueva constitución política del estado*. UPS, La Paz.

Fine, B. (1999). The developmental state is dead: Long live social capital? *Development and Change*, *30*(1), 1–19.

Fung, A., Wright, E. O., & Abers, R. (2003). *Deepening democracy: Institutional innovations in empowered participatory governance*. Verso.

Gaventa, J. (2004). Towards participatory governance: Assessing the transformative possibilities. In B. Cooke & U. Kothari (Eds.), *Participation: The new tyranny?* Zed Books.

Green, M. (2010). Making development agents: Participation as boundary object in international development. *The Journal of Development Studies*, *46*(7), 1240–1263. https://doi.org/10.1080/00220388.2010.487099

Guijt, I., & Shah, M. K. (1998). *The myth of community: Gender issues in participatory development*. IT Publications.

Harten, S. (2011). *The rise of Evo Morales and the MAS*. ZED Books.

Heller, P. (2001). Moving the state: The politics of democratic decentralization in Kerala, South Africa, and Porto Alegre. *Politics & Society*, *29*, 131–163.

Henkel, H., Stirrat, R., Wolvekamp, P., & Reddy, S. (2001). Participation as spiritual duty: Empowerment as secular subjection. In B. Cooke & U. Kothari (Eds.), *Participation: The new tyranny?* Zed Books.

Hesketh, C., & Morton, A. D. (2014). Spaces of uneven development and class struggle in Bolivia: Transformation or trasformismo? *Antipode*, *46*(1), 149–169. https://doi.org/10.1111/anti.12038

Hickey, S., & Mohan, G. (2005). Relocating participation within a radical politics of development. *Development and Change*, *36*, 237–262.

Hildyard, N., Hegde, P., Wolvekamp, P., & Reddy, S. (2001). Pluralism, participation and power: Joint forest management. In B. Cooke & U. Kothari (Eds.), *Participation: The new tyranny?* (pp. 56–71). ZED Books.

Hippert, C. (2011). Women's spaces, gender mainstreaming, and development priorities: Popular participation as gendered work in rural Bolivia. *Women's Studies International Forum*, *34*, 498–508.

INE (Instituto Nacional de Estadísticas), Estado Plurinacional de Bolivia. (2014). Censo Nacional de Población y Vivienda. *Statistics*. www.ine.gov.bo

Kesby, M. (2005). Retheorizing empowerment-through-participation as a performance in space: Beyond tyranny to transformation. *Signs*, *30*(4), 2037–2065. https://doi.org/10.1086/428422

Kindon, S. L., Pain, R., & Kesby, M. (2007). *Participatory action research approaches and methods: Connecting people, participation and place*. Routledge.

Kohl, B. H. (2003). Democratizing decentralization in Bolivia. *Journal of Planning Education and Research, 23*(2), 153–164. https://doi.org/10.1177/0739456X03258639

Kohl, B. H., & Farthing, L. (2006). *Impasse in Bolivia: Neoliberal hegemony and popular resistance*. ZED Books.

Kohl, B. H., & Farthing, L. (2012). Material constraints to popular imaginaries: The extractive economy and resource nationalism in Bolivia. *Political Geography*, *31*, 225–235.

Komadina, J. (2009). Las tribulaciones del control social. *Opinión*.

Kothari, U., & Hickey, S. (2009). Participation. In *International encyclopedia of human geography*. Elsevier Science & Technology Books.

Según el oficialismo, el artículo 241 acercar los poderes al pueblo. El control social vigilar a al Estado. (2009). *La Rázon*.

Larson, B. (1988). *Colonialism and agrarian transformation in Bolivia: Cochabamba, 1550–1900*. Princeton University Press.

Lazar, S. (2007). *El Alto, Rebel City: Self and citizenship in Andean Bolivia* (W. D. Mignolo, I. Silverblatt, & S. Saldívar-Hull, Eds.). Duke University Press. https://doi.org/10.1215/9780822388760

Leal, P. A. (2007). Participation: The ascendancy of a buzzword in the neo-liberal era. *Development in Practice*, *17*(4–5), 539–548. https://doi.org/10.1080/09614520701469518

Lister, R. (1998). Citizen in action: Citizenship and community development in Northern Ireland context. *Community Development Journal*, *33*(3), 226–235.

Long, C. (2001). *Participation of the poor in development initiatives: Taking their rightful places*. Earthscan Publications.

Mansuri, G., & Rao, V. (2013). *Localizing development: Does participation work?, Policy research report*. World Bank.

Masaki, K. (2004). The "transformative" unfolding of "tyrannical" participation: The corvée tradition and ongoing local politics in Western Nepal. In S. Hickey & G. Mohan (Eds.), *Participation: From tyranny to transformation?: Exploring new approaches to participation in development*. ZED Books.

McNeish, J.-A. (2013). Extraction, protest and indigeneity in Bolivia: The TIPNIS effect. *Latin American and Caribbean Ethnic Studies*, *8*(2), 221–242. https://doi.org/10.1080/17442222.2013.808495

Medina Hoyos, T. (2009). Constitución y control social. *Opinión*.

Mehta, L. (2001). The manufacture of popular perceptions of scarcity: Dams and water-related narratives in Gujarat, India. *World Development*, *29*(12), 2025–2041. https://doi.org/10.1016/S0305-750X(01)00087-0

Midgley, J. (1986). *Community participation, social development, and the state*. Methuen.

Miraftab, F. (2006). Feminist praxis, citizenship and informal politics: Reflections on South Africa's anti-eviction campaign. *International Feminist Journal of Politics*, *8*(2), 194–218. https://doi.org/10.1080/14616740600612830

Mohan, G., & Stokke, K. (2000). Participatory development and empowerment: The dangers of localism. *Third World Quarterly*, *21*(2), 247–268. https://doi.org/10.1080/01436590050004346

Moreno, K. (2009, March 12). El Control Social. *La Rázon*.

Mosse, D. (2003). The making and marketing of participatory development. In P. Quarles van Ufford & A. Kumar Giri (Eds.), *A moral critique of development: In search of global responsibilities*. Institut for Historie, Internationale Studier og Samfundsforhold, Aalborg Universitet.

Olivera, M. (2014). Water beyond the state. *NACLA: Report on the Americas*, *47*(3), 64–68.

Osmani, S. R. (2000). *Participatory governance, people's empowerment and poverty reduction*. United Nations Development Programme.

Pacto de Unidad. (2007). *Propuesta consensuada del pacto de unidad*. Constitución política del estado Boliviano.

Pellegrini, L. (2012). Planning and natural resources in Bolivia: Between rules without participation and participation without rules. *Journal of Developing Societies*, *28*(2), 185–202. https://doi.org/10.1177/0169796X12448757

Perreault, T. (2015). Performing participation: Mining, power, and the limits of public consultation in Bolivia. *The Journal of Latin American and Caribbean Anthropology*, *20*(3), 433–451. https://doi.org/10.1111/jlca.12185

Postero, N. (2010). The struggle to create a radical democracy in Bolivia. *Latin American Research Review*, *45*, 59–78, 336–337.

Postero, N. (2017). *The Indigenous state: Race, politics and performance in plurinational Bolivia*. University of California Press.

Pretty, J. (2008). Agricultural sustainability: Concepts, principles and evidence. *Philosophical Transactions of the Royal Society of London: Series B, Biological Sciences*, *363*(1491), 447–465. https://doi.org/10.1098/rstb.2007.2163

Pretty, J., & Hine, R. (1999). *Participatory appraisal for community assessment*. Centre for Environment and Society, University of Essex.

Probst, K., & Hagmann, J. (2003). Understanding participatory research in the context of natural resource management: Paradigms, approaches and typologies. *ODI Agicultural Research & Extension Network, Network Paper No. 130.*

Regalsky, P. (2010). Political processes and the reconfiguration of the state in Bolivia. *Latin American Perspectives, 37*(3), 35–50.

Regalsky, P., & Laurie, N. (2007). "The school, whose place is this"? The deep structures of the hidden curriculum in indigenous education in Bolivia. *Comparative Education, 43*(2), 231–251. https://doi.org/10.1080/03050060701362482

Rivera Cusicanqui, S. (2010). *Violencias (re)encubiertas en Bolivia.* La Mirada Salvaje/Editorial Piedra Rota.

Sánchez, F. (2008, October 14). Contradiciones constitucionales: Control social y justicia comunitaria. *El Diario.*

Saxena, N. C. (2011). What is meant by people's participation? In A. Cornwall (Ed.), *The participation reader* (pp. 31–33). ZED Books; Distributed in the USA exclusively by Palgrave Macmillan.

Stefanoni, P. (2007). Bolivia, bajo el signo del nacionalismo indígena: seis preguntas y seis respuestas sobre el gobierno de Evo Morales. In K. Monasterios, P. Stefanoni, & H. Do Alto (Eds.), *Reinventando la nación en Bolivia.* CLASCO/Plural.

Stiefel, M., & Wolfe, M. (1994). *A voice for the excluded: Popular participation in development: Utopia or necessity?* Zed Books.

Torrico, E., Canedo, G., Torrico, C., & Ventura, G. (2013). *Villas rebeldes: apuntes sobre las organizaciones vecinales de la periferie urbana en Bolivia.* CEDIB.

Urioste, M., & Baldomar, L. (1996). Ley de Participación Popular: Seguimiento crítico. In Rojas Ortuste (Ed.), *La Participación Pupular: Avances y obstaculos (report of the Secretaria de Participación Popular, Ministerio de Desarollo Humano, Bolivia).* grupo DRU/SNPP.

Waddington, M., & Mohan, G. (2004). Failing forward: Going beyond PRA and imposed forms of participation. In S. Hickey & G. Mohan (Eds.), *Participation: From tyranny to transformation?: Exploring new approaches to participation in development.* ZED Books.

Webber, J. R. (2010). Struggle, continuity, and contradiction in Bolivia. *International Socialism, 125,* np. http://isj.org.uk/struggle-continuity-and-contradiction-in-bolivia/ (accessed March 29, 2019).

Webber, J. R. (2011). *From rebellion to reform in Bolivia: Class struggle, Indigenous liberation, and the politics of Evo Morales.* Haymarket Books.

White, S. (2011). Depoliticizing development: The uses and abuses of participation. In A. Cornwall (Ed.), *The participation reader* (pp. 57–69). ZED Books.

Williams, G. (2004). Towards a repoliticization of participatory development: Political capabilities and spaces of empowerment. In S. Hickey & G. Mohan (Eds.), *Participation: From tyranny to transformation?: Exploring new approaches to participation in development.* ZED Books.

World Bank. (1997). *The state in a changing world: World development report.* Oxford University Press.

World Bank. (2000). *PRSP sourcebook.* World Bank.

Zegada, M. T., Arce, C., Canedo, G., & Quispe, A. (2011). *La democracia desde los márgenes: Transformaciones en el campo politico boliviano.* CLASCO; Muela del Diablo Editores.

4 *"Semapa es de los Cochabambinos"*

Participation and social control in the Cochabamba water sector

This chapter continues the account of participation and social control in Bolivia with an examination of participatory water governance in the city of Cochabamba. It applies the framework developed in the previous chapter to the water sector in Cochabamba, revealing that the outcomes of participation can indeed differ from the intents and that conflicting forms of participation have created tensions amongst water users, policy makers, and activists in the city.

I first look at the period of privatization of Cochabamba's water services as a prominent example of reformative participation. I then turn to the more transformative forms of participation that can be observed in the water movement that culminated in the Water War that rejected privatization and demanded water services be returned to the public sphere. The concept of social control that emerged from the water movement at this time centred around this demand and the resolve to democratize the water system through greater citizen involvement in governance (Aguilar Miranda & Miranda Hernández, 2012). The Water War can also be understood as a catalyst for broader change in Bolivia, sparking further resource wars and a shift to the left with the election of Evo Morales and the MAS party in December 2005, assuming office in January 2006. Morales responded to water sector demands with the formal recognition of the Right to Water as well as the traditional model of uses and customs. New state institutions dedicated to water management were created at the national level, notably a Water Ministry, which incorporated mechanisms of participation and social control. I argue that although these formal mechanisms were based on transformative participation demands that grew out of popular unrest, they have resulted in nominal practices that have served to work against meaningful change. The attention paid to social control in the formal water sector has largely been rhetorical, with contradictions between official discourse and practice.

The participatory efforts implemented in Cochabamba's municipal water company, Semapa, did not transfer decision-making control to the

DOI: 10.4324/9781003169383-4

population, thereby maintaining a power imbalance between marginalized users and management in municipal services. Despite the institutionalization of participation and social control, Semapa has not been very transparent, remains unaccountable to Cochabambinos, and continues to be used as a tool for political gain by local politicians. Tensions between different conceptions of participation and social control, institutional inertia, and lingering market conventions within the water sector have prevented the establishment of a progressive public water system. Transformative participation in the water sector can be found, however, at the community scale in Cochabamba, as seen in the case of alternative housing collective Maria Auxiliadora, an example of grassroots practices of inclusive participation.

Water privatization and reformative participation

The privatization of Cochabamba's water utility formed part of the wave of neoliberal restructuring in Bolivia that applied market logic to improve inefficiencies in public services. By the 1990s, privatization had become a precondition to borrowing from major financial donors (Goldman, 2007). Indeed, in 1996, the World Bank threatened to deny $600 million in debt relief if the Bolivian government did not privatize the water sector (Dangl, 2007). At this time, popular participation mechanisms had been introduced through the Law of Popular Participation to provide the supposed social stability needed to attract private investors (Ahlers, 2005). As such, the participation sought under water privatization can be understood as reformative, with the intent to use participation as a tool to expand market access. In line with neoliberal pro-poor policies, people participate as customers in a "transition" from poverty.

The municipal company Samapa, in La Paz/El Alto, was the first water service to be granted a concession to Aguas del Illimani, a consortium led by French transnational Suez, in 1997 (Barja Daza & Urquiola, 2005). Cochabamba's water system, Semapa, was targeted next. In a city of close to half a million residents, the water system was critically over-capacity and viewed as a textbook example of the public sector's inability to properly administer basic services. Nevertheless, the first bidding process was unsuccessful and the second, two years later under Hugo Banzer's administration, produced a sole bidder, led by the engineering conglomerate Bechtel, based in San Francisco. The 40-year concession contract was signed under the Bechtel consortium, Aguas del Tunari, on 3 September 1999.

Apart from multinationals, local elites often support and benefit from privatization (Conaghan & Malloy, 1994). In the Cochabamba case, the sale was advantageous to Bolivian companies who owned 20% of the consortium shares (Spronk & Crespo, 2008, np).[1] Aguas del Tunari did not take over operations until November 1999 when Potable Water and Sanitation Law 2029 passed. The law eliminated basic service subsidies and enforced the commercialization of water and the privatization of municipal water systems (Ahlers, 2005; Assies, 2003). Further, the law allocated water rights to multinational companies for use towards mining, agriculture, and electricity, while prohibitively limiting alternative water distribution systems (Crespo et al., 2004). The law corresponded to French-style concession contracts, widespread in Latin America at the time, spanning from 25 to 40 years (Budds & McGranahan, 2003). Accordingly, multinationals were granted exclusive provision of sanitation services for 40 years, whereas independent water committees, cooperatives, and communal systems were only granted temporary licenses for five years (Law 2029).

Aguas del Tunari also had the right to seize water sources in their concession zone, which included water sources used by the various small-scale systems in Cochabamba's peripheral Southern Zone as well as irrigating farmers' sources in the surrounding rural areas. The concession also included exclusive use of water resources in the Cochabamba Valley, the largest irrigated area in Bolivia (Assies, 2003). The communities reliant upon small-scale water systems as well as irrigating farmers were thus prompted to mobilize against privatization, though they had no direct connections to the municipal service. They were interested in rescinding the contract and reversing the law that granted monopoly rights on water sources traditionally used collectively (Bustamante et al., 2005).

The scale of the irrigation networks and the complexity involved in expanding the water system to encompass self-managed water systems only became clear to Aguas del Tunari after the contract was signed (Paniagua, Interview, 2014). The costs of the projected expansion were offloaded onto the urban residents connected to the service, and, as a result, user fees skyrocketed to unaffordable levels, in some cases with increases of up to 200% (Olivera & Lewis, 2004). The next section describes how these different sectors united against privatization, forming a movement to reaffirm social control of water systems and demonstrating how neoliberal reformative participation plans failed to provide the stability intended by the Law of Popular Participation.

The Water War and social control as counter-narrative

The privatization of Cochabamba's water services provoked a broad mobilization of Cochabamba residents, who took to the streets for several months of protest, culminating in eight days of intense confrontation in early April 2000 (for extensive accounts of the Water War days see Bakker, 2010; Crespo et al., 2004; Laurie, 2011; Olivera & Lewis, 2004; Shultz, 2008; here the focus will be on the calls for participation and social control). These events, known as Cochabamba's Water War, are commonly upheld as a model of successful anti-privatization mobilization, as the private contract for the city's water was ultimately rescinded. The demands for social control made during the Water War were conceived as a way to widen the scope of democratic control over public services and the use of resources. Water as a vehicle for political change and social control became the counter-narrative to reformative participation from the neoliberal order. Indeed, the Water War sparked a cycle of left–Indigenous revolt in the country that informed the Water War and Gas Wars in La Paz-El Alto, resulting in the resignations of Sánchez de Lozada and Carlos Mesa and the eventual election of MAS and Evo Morales.

As noted, rural residents of Cochabamba were opposed to the monopoly rights stipulated in Law 2029 and the contract that would grant Aguas del Tunari rights to exploit what the Cochabambinos viewed as their water sources, which were already highly contested from earlier conflicts. In the late 1970s, Semapa drilled wells in the neighbouring town of Quillacollo in an attempt to provide water to the city of Cochabamba. This manoeuvre dried up wells used by the town's residents and gave rise to protests. Drilling outside the city was proposed once more after a severe water shortage in the 1990s, this time giving rise to the *Guerra de los Pozos* (War of the Wells), a series of conflicts in 1998 between Semapa and irrigating farmers from rural areas surrounding the city (Crespo, 1999). One result of these conflicts was the formation of Cochabamba's Federation of Irrigators, FEDECOR, part of an autonomous popular movement in defence of traditional Indigenous communitarian uses and customs. The federation, an organized base of irrigating farmers well versed in water legislation, played a pivotal role in the Water War of 2000. In fact, their reaction to Law 2029 made them the "early risers" in the movement for public control of the water systems against market interests (Tarrow, 1994, as cited in Assies, 2003, p. 51).

The residents of the peri-urban Southern Zone of Cochabamba, who were also not connected to the water utility, now found themselves within the Aguas del Tunari concession zone. The independent small-scale systems and the water sources they relied upon were now under threat of expropriation by foreign capital. These communities felt ownership over their systems as they put time, effort, and their savings into these systems in absence of state support. The Aguas del Tunari contract stipulated that the consortium would upgrade the networks and expand infrastructure to reach the population not serviced by the utility, yet no improvements materialized under privatization. Spikes in water tariffs affected people indiscriminately, thus creating a wider base for organizing the mobilizations. The coalition that formed between rural and urban residents, *La Coordinadora*, acted as a mouthpiece for the people and became the base for organizing. Following the most critical days in April 2000 of heightened police violence and relentless protest, the contract was cancelled. The irrigators held barricades outside of the city, blocking major transportation routes, until Law 2029, which permitted privatization, was reversed. The popular water movement united around three key related notions: water cannot be sold and privatization should be banished; reclaiming social control of water management; and a defence of traditional uses and customs.

The negative impacts of privatization and the experience of the Water War firmly entrenched an anti-privatization sentiment for many Cochabamba residents who rose to defend water as a public resource, because they viewed it as an essential element for agricultural production and for life. Water has a unique and symbolic value attached to it as a productive resource but also as a spiritual source of life and a human and environmental right (Bennett, 1995). According to the "Water Warriors," the Water War activists, local water supplies form part of the commons and should not be available for commercialization by foreign corporations or the Bolivian state. The emphasis shifted to public ownership over water and, more specifically, to community ownership where water resources are governed under communal water rights and collective provision of irrigation (Narain, 2006; Shiva, 2002).

Motivated by the lack of transparency during the privatization process, public participation and social control of the water utility became the alternative to an opaque system. Thus, the main demand emerging from the grassroots Water War mobilization in Cochabamba was the democratization of decision-making in water management. The implementation of social control provided an alternative to privatization as well as a remedy to the problems of previous state models of water management that ultimately facilitated privatization. Through participation and collective action, the citizens of Cochabamba managed to oust a major multinational from their city; so, it followed that participation would be a demand towards positive changes within the newly reinstated Semapa. According to Oscar Olivera, one of the key organizers of the anti-privatization protests, the Water War was about achieving universal access and adequate sanitation services and ensuring that unaffordable tariff increases would not reoccur. This goal would be achieved by gaining control over the decisions that affect people's livelihoods, making social control and public participation a fundamental issue:

> La Coordinadora's demands were not strictly demands about management; they were demands that were more political, beyond the management of water. One of the fundamental demands was a substantial change in the economic model of privatization that was implemented in Bolivia, and a change in the policy, that is, that everything is regulated,

that is established as a type of norm, not only of coexistence, issues of the actual functioning of the institutional state structures, are not a privilege or monopoly of the few, of political parties, of business owners; that they are a model of political participation, audit, and decisions that matter to the people that they affect.

(O. Olivera, Interview, 2014)[2]

The demand for participation is reflected on the international scale as well in the proceedings following the Water War. In 2002, as a result of the contract cancellation, Bechtel filed a $25 million lawsuit against the Bolivian government for breach of contract and loss of profits based on the bilateral investment treaty with the International Centre for Settlement of Investment Disputes run by the World Bank (Goldman, 2007). An international movement launched a public campaign for Bechtel to drop the lawsuit; this included a petition for transparency and to allow public participation in the court proceedings—typically held in camera (Spronk & Crespo, 2008). Due to public pressure, the suit was dropped in 2004 in exchange for a symbolic sum of money paid to the multinational by the Bolivian government (Spronk & Crespo, 2008). This presented another victory against foreign capital and reinforced the potency of public participation.

During the Water War, the concept of *usos y costumbres*, or uses and customs, was championed as an alternative to the privatization model. According to *usos y costumbres*, water governance is decided amongst the people through mutually agreed upon arrangements based on people's needs rather than profit motives. This emphasis on people-centred governance offers an example of a transformative participation model. Garande and Dagg (2005) reference Michener's (1998) argument that people-centred participation empowers people or community when there is collective consciousness-raising, "enhance[d] local management capacity," and greater "confidence in Indigenous potential" (p. 420). *Usos y costumbres*, grounded in Andean principles of reciprocity and redistribution (Bustamante & Gutiérrez, 1999), can be based on Indigenous traditions even when community members might not explicitly identify as Indigenous.[3] Here, empowerment lies in the fact that community members are involved in the decision-making process through participatory assemblies and the democratic selection of leaders. Although not without flaws, the emphasis on public participation among self-governed systems in the Southern Zone provided a model of water governance that Cochabambinos could uphold.

Returning to the idea that communities felt ownership over their existing water systems, they were outraged that a private company could expropriate the systems and the water sources that "belonged" to them. This points to Cleaver's (2001, p. 51) distinction between autonomy as an "expression of agency" or a "necessity imposed by constraint." Initially, the self-governed systems were formed due to the lack of municipal services (constraint), but, following the threat of privatization, the emphasis on protecting autonomy and upholding traditional water rights that emerged can be understood as a demonstration of agency. This is evidenced by the formation of ASICA-Sur, now known as ASICA-SUDD-EPSAS (Departmental Association of Community Water Systems of the South and Provider Entities of Water and Sanitation Services), an umbrella network of Southern Zone water committees. The protection of these systems (especially against the threat of privatization) became an important point of mobilization, as they provided an alternative to market-driven forms of water governance.

These three ideas—that water cannot be commercialized, public participation and social control is critical, and a defence of *usos y costumbres*—formed the basis for the water movement's vision for the restructuring of Semapa:

> Of course there are many problems to be faced; however, the challenge accepted in April by the population as a whole, and by *La Coordinadora* especially, is to consolidate a company of potable water and sewage that **maintains its public character, under control of the population and moreover, that is efficient, that has the capacity to improve and expand its services whose operation is transparent.** To achieve this goal it is necessary to consolidate a management model of Semapa that facilitates the active participation of the organized population in the design of general policies and decision-making, and what's more, that permits the audit of company activities by grassroots organizations.
>
> (*Coordinadora*, 2001, np, emphasis in the original)

> Therefore, over the past seven months, in the transition of the previous Semapa managed as "political booty"—originating in political patronage, fiscal irrationality, corruption and political interference that allowed for losses in efficiency and efficacy—to a Semapa that responds to the mandate of the population . . . to structure services in which citizens assume a role not only of simple users or benefactors, but the role of concrete actors in the organization, administration, and control of a company that is efficient, that is, to resolve the problems of provision of water and sewage services/sanitation in adequate quantity and quality, that is productive and efficient, that is, that provides those services at reasonable costs expressed in a just tariff system.
>
> (*Coordinadora*, 2001, np)

La Coordinadora made explicit calls for public participation and social control with the expectation that these measures could solve or at the least help address the various problems within Semapa that predated—and made the company a target for—privatization. However, this vision faced push-back from the outset.

Nominal participation normalized

Two decades after the Water War, Semapa uses the tagline "clear and transparent," but in reality this is far from true. During my fieldwork, I spent time at the Semapa offices to understand how public participation and social control are operationalized. In October 2014, I attended the biannual *Audiencia publica de rendición de cuentas*, a public accountability hearing. These meetings are structured as an hour-long presentation followed by a 15-minute question and answer period, organized by Semapa's Transparency Unit. The room was half full; the majority in attendance were Semapa workers complying with their work obligations, and there were 14 members of the public, who were mostly community representatives. Available records from previous and subsequent meetings denote the same poor attendance rate.[4] In discussion with community leaders—*dirigentes*, heads of water committees and cooperatives in the Southern Zone—many were unaware of the meeting dates and had not received the letter of invitation. Instead, they lamented the lack of communication from Semapa. One *dirigente* pointed to a stack of unanswered letters of complaint.

Aside from the poor promotion of the meeting, the scheduling is also problematic. Held mid-morning on a Wednesday, the busiest market day of the week after Saturday, the meeting time conflicts with most work schedules. Furthermore, Semapa's headquarters are located in uptown Cochabamba, which typically requires a one-hour commute from the Southern districts, depending on traffic. Location and timing present accessibility challenges. Additionally, public records of meeting minutes are not shared widely. The meeting itself consisted of an information session of mission statements, overviews of the year's projects, and general financial information presented by various Semapa managers, who occasionally stopped to answer their cell phones. For the question and answer session, the attendees were not given the floor; rather, questions were submitted on paper to be read out by a Semapa representative. The different managers would then answer the questions, often deflecting problems, and quickly moved on to the next question without leaving time for deliberation or discussion. There were a total of eight questions that were answered within 12 minutes. This is the heft of the current mechanism for social control and public participation.

These meetings do not amount to the robust public engagement called for during the Water War of 2000. Far from observing meaningful exchange, the mechanisms in place today reflect nominal participation promoted in rhetoric only. Here, public decision-making is contained to exclusive circles, and participation is a display of public meetings whereby the water utility can claim they are fulfilling their obligation to public participation and social control. This kind of nominal participation has become normalized in formal spaces of the Bolivian water sector at the municipal, departmental, and national levels.

This returns to the central question of the book: What prevented transformative participation from taking hold? My research uncovers four key interrelating barriers. The first issue is the divide in perspectives on the meanings of public and participation. Resistance to transformative participation made it difficult to rebuild a different Semapa. This informs the next factor: lacking strong participatory mechanisms, institutional inertia took hold as corruption and political influence plagued Semapa. Third is the contradiction between the discourse and the actions of Evo Morales and the MAS government, which captured the idea of participation and social control to reproduce clientelist relationships and restricted access to higher-level decision-making. Finally, buttressed by government inconsistency and complacency, lasting neoliberal logic presents a challenge to transformative participation. I explore each of these four factors in turn in the following.

Defining the "new" Semapa: Early divides

Directly following the Water War, Semapa reverted to an autonomous decentralized public utility that was temporarily reconstituted as "*Semapa Residual*" (residual in Spanish). The conservative national government of Hugo Banzer was in power, but the task to rebuild Semapa occurred at the local level, with the New Republic Force (NFR—*Nueva Fuerza Republicana*), a centre-right party in the mayor's office (Sánchez Gómez & Terhorst, 2005). *Semapa Residual* was headed by a Board of Directors that consisted of municipal officials. The population of Cochabamba was dissatisfied with this return to the former state model that had been riddled with problems. Moreover, they were distrustful of this Board because of their involvement in the utility's privatization—they had not only endorsed the concession contract but also supported Aguas del Tunari in claiming economic losses for breach of contract and their forced exit from Bolivia. The search for an alternative model of water management was not a straightforward process, however.

La Coordinadora remained active following the Water War, holding consultations and workshops to put together a proposal for Semapa's restructuring. *La Coordinadora* understood participation and social control as a way to improve the public entity so it would not be a target for privatization (Wainwright, 2012, p. 88): "The true opposite to privatization is the social re-appropriation of wealth by working-class society itself—self-organized in communal structure of management, in neighbourhood associations, in unions, and in the rank and file" (Oscar Olivera quoted in Spronk, 2009, p. 27). The push towards democratizing public services was important for all sectors of the population, even those not connected to the municipal network, because it was linked to struggles over natural resources (Crespo, 2006, p. 4). *La Coordinadora*'s initial proposal called to dissolve state property and replace the utility structures as common property (Coordinadora, 2001). However, the idea of Semapa as common property was viewed as too radical and *La Coordinadora* members preemptively modified the proposal to be more palatable.

The second proposal was penned by the College of Professionals of Cochabamba, a group composed of professionals across 17 fields that were involved in some way in the Water War. This group had strong ties to the mayor's office, and their proposal included input from Semapa workers (Crespo & Orellana, 2004). Finally, a third proposal was presented by the *junta vecinal*, a neighbourhood council that was also aligned with the municipality.

As laid out in Table 4.1, the key differentiating factor between the three proposals is the amount and type of participation. *La Coordinadora*'s proposal exemplifies a model of water management often referred to locally as public–social that would place decisions about the water utility directly in the citizen representatives' control. With six social representatives, the public would hold a majority vote on the Board of Directors that would be held accountable through public assemblies. The other two proposals conceived public participation quite differently, placing Semapa firmly under government control, with social representatives forming a minority on the Board of Directors. This composition allowed for civil society input without granting final decision-making power. According to my earlier categorization of participation, these state-led spaces do not automatically preclude transformative participation, but in Cochabamba it is often tied to a paternalistic view of social control that persists today, as exemplified by this quote from a former manager at Semapa:

[Participation] is a way to administer the state that I do not agree with much. . . . I consider this country one that has not reached maturity of First World countries of hundreds or thousands of years of democracy. Are you going to consult an immature [country], what decision will it take? One example, I have three children, who are now grown, but when they were younger, what would they like to eat today? One will say chicken, the other hamburgers, and the other will say "I want ice cream." But ice cream is not nourishment. Second, I cannot cook three different things, and third, my budget does not allow it, I only have enough for eggs and rice. So why ask?

(Former General Manager of Semapa, Interview, 2014)

Table 4.1 Three proposals for Semapa's new statute

	La Coordinadora	College of Professionals	Junta vecinal
Proposed composition of Semapa's board of directors	6 Social representatives (elected via direct vote) 2 Municipal representatives 1 Semapa union representative 1 General manager	2 Representatives of the water user council 1 Representative of the technical council 2 Municipal representatives 1 Technical prefecture representative 1 Engineering society representative 1 General manager	3 Social representatives 2 Municipal representatives 1 Semapa union representative 1 Engineering society representative 1 Representative Vigilance committee
Other specifications	• Public hearings • Citizen consultations • Recall election/referendum mandate	• Tariff increases will not require public consultations • No confidential vote for social representatives	• Public hearings • No confidential neighbourhood vote, elect leaders from each neighbourhood • No recall election/referendum mandate

(Adapted from Crespo & Fernández, 2004, p. 41)

In other words, technical experts are seen in this model to be better suited to address water issues than the average citizen. Here, the "technical problem" of water scarcity requires "technical solutions," which, in Cochabamba, have been modernist projects such as the Misicuni Dam construction, where public input is not as valued.

A new statute for Semapa was approved on 25 October 2001. In the end, the outcome of the citizens' directory was a much less radical version than what was envisioned by *La Coordinadora*. The composition of the board was three citizen representatives from different districts of Cochabamba, two representatives from the municipal government, one from the College of Professionals, and one union representative. With a minority of citizen representatives serving on the Board of Directors, the participatory criteria of "inclusion" was fulfilled but not that of "control."

Several factors contributed to the inability of the water movement to achieve its initial demands. By the time discussions around restructuring Semapa with social control were solidifying a year after the Water War, *La Coordinadora* had lost mobilization power (Crespo & Orellana, 2004). It had waned because actors were preoccupied with different regional and national movements. For instance, the irrigators' movement, once the main instigator of water proposals, had shifted their focus solely to irrigators' issues. Also, several of the informal leaders of *La Coordinadora* were beginning to shift their commitment away from water issues in order position themselves politically to align with MAS (Crespo, Interview, 2014). With decreased numbers, maintaining pressure on the municipality to achieve demands proved difficult (Driessen, 2008). *La Coordinadora* fostered unity during the Water War by identifying a common enemy, the privatization of water services, which allowed people to band together regardless of socio-economic standing. The distinct motivations people had for joining the Water War protests—protecting water sources, guarding autonomous water systems, and fighting against rising tariffs—did not translate to a consensus going forward in the restructuring of Semapa. *La Coordinadora*'s initial ideas were viewed as too radical and were thus tempered in order to achieve a modicum of social control incorporated into the utility's management (Spronk, 2007).

Further, the water movement was challenged by the resistance of elite actors, particularly within the municipal government, who wanted to preserve Semapa as a tool for political gain (Driessen, 2008). An unlikely alliance of this local elite was the Semapa workers' union, whose interference was detrimental to the restructuring process (Sánchez Gómez & Terhorst, 2005), with the union leadership, aligning itself with the administration's stance on maintaining the previous management model (Wainwright, 2012). The water workers lobbied to preserve their role of relative power, thus limiting the number of citizen representatives (Crespo & Orellana, 2004). Although Semapa workers were part of the movement that pushed out Aguas del Tunari, they notably did not seek *La Coordinadora*'s representation like other trade unions. *La Coordinadora* could not rely on their support, limiting their ability to form connections with water users and Cochabamba communities and transform the company from within. As Oscar Olivera (Interview, 2014) attests:

> Both [the general manager and the union] united to impede any type of internal restructuring of the company that would permit an opening for people's participation in the company. For me, like I said, this addition was missing, but what's more, for me it's an absolute lack of reciprocity and gratitude from the workers and administrators of the company towards the people that made the recuperation of the company, thanks to the collective force of the people. . . . They lost perspective, the historical vision of the compromise they should take on with the people, that in 2000 the company was recuperated for the people, not only for themselves.

Wainwright (2012) points out the importance of examining the organization of labour and "human relations" to see how the relationships can contribute to democratizing public institutions. She argues that relations between labour and management are "decisive to the flows of information, knowledge, and problem solving among staff and between staff and users," and that the "combination is vital to achieving the goals, the measurements and the dynamics of a different kind of economic logic" (Wainwright, 2012, p. 88). Despite the terse history of cooperation between management, workers, and users, there have been instances of worker-led, management-supported collaboration. However, in the crucial moments following the Water War, *La Coordinadora* could not rely on the full support of Semapa workers, a considerable blow to the water movement.

While *La Coordinadora's* initial ideas did not materialize, they did manage to ensure some mechanisms of social control within Semapa. They pushed to include a Vigilance and Social Control Unit within the company, with the function of investigating instances of corruption and tracking inefficiencies. The unit was meant to be independent and consist of Semapa workers and civil society (Sánchez Gómez & Terhorst, 2005, p. 125). This unit took years to approve and was eventually established within Semapa as the Transparency Unit, mandated by the Ministry of Transparency, to deal with complaints that correspond to Semapa. *La Coordinadora* was also able to secure their proposed statute for citizen directors to be approved by the Board of Directors (Crespo & Orellana, 2004). The following responsibilities of citizen directors were included in Article 15 of the statute: 1) present trimestral reports to water committees; 2) call emergency meetings in the event of a tariff raise or change in tariff structure; 3) propose water and sewage improvement projects in coordination with communities; 4) attend meetings called by the Board of Directors; 5) support the organization of basic sanitation workshops and training sessions; 6) survey the quality of services; and 7) encourage users to pay bills. The regulations for citizen representative elections were passed 23 February 2002 (Crespo & Orellana, 2004).

Institutional inertia

The limited mechanisms for participation and social control of citizen representatives faced problems from the first elections of a new Semapa Board of Directors. These were held in April 2002, the same year as the national general elections. People were not as motivated about water issues as they had been two years previously, however, and more importantly, most were preoccupied with the larger elections. With minimal publicity, the mayor sent last minute notice of the Semapa representatives election, to be held prior to the Departmental elections (Crespo & Orellana, 2004). Moreover, voters were identified through a database of ELFEC users (the electric utility company *Empresa de Luz y Fuerza Électrica Cochabamba*), limiting the vote to one per family (the person whose name appears on the bill), thereby circumventing the participation of tenants who do not pay the electricity bill directly. The motivation behind this approach is not clear (Crespo & Orellana, 2004). The elections garnered 597 votes from the Northern Zone, 648 votes in the Central Zone, and 1,935 votes from the Southern Zone for a total of 3,174 votes or 3.6% of eligible voters (Crespo & Orellana, 2004, p. 48). Even with this low voter turnout the elections were contested due to disorganized voting stations, and accounts abound of people being told where to mark the ballot by Semapa workers and those administering the vote. Recall elections were held, but subsequent elections remained problematic.

Once holding positions, the citizen representatives received little to no training on how to communicate with the public or methods to evaluate Semapa's plans and operations. Graver still was the ability of other members of the Board of Directors to politically influence the citizen representatives. Due to their marginalized position of minority vote, citizen representatives often limited themselves to petitioning for improvements in their neighbourhoods of the city alone. Other times, they would vote in favour of the Board in exchange for positions at Semapa for friends and family (Crespo & Orellana, 2004). At worst, citizen representatives were directly offered financial compensation in exchange for their vote or silence regarding corruption (Former Citizen Representative, Interview, 2014).

By 2010, the positions of citizen representatives on the Board of Directors quietly dissolved. Semapa was no longer holding elections for these posts and no one protested (Rodriguez, Interview, 2014). People lost faith in the ability of citizen representatives to change the internal dynamics of Semapa. In short, it was a failed experiment because it did not provide a strong voice for the public, as decision-making power was not transferred to the citizens of Cochabamba. The momentum of the water movement had weakened, and with diminished social pressure, Semapa had returned to the status quo prior to privatization, a vehicle for corruption and political gain, ultimately having adverse effects on network improvements and expansions.

Also present is the problem of institutional instability, linked to the high turnover rate of General Managers in Semapa. They are appointed by the mayor and typically serve one to two years heading the company (which itself is insufficient for a sector like water with long-term time horizons), though some periods have seen up to five changes in General Manager in one year (Chaquicallata, Interview, 2014). For those who wanted to make shifts in Semapa, two years was not enough, and if they initiated too many changes their term could be cut short, as noted by one former General Manager:

> Semapa has always been used politically, without any importance given to the wellbeing of the population. . . . My commitment was to be the General Manager for two years. To stop the corruption in Semapa. . . . The first step was accomplished. I let go 152 workers. There was a 15-day strike, there were blockades, they beat me in the streets. Never has this been done in Semapa. Why? Because there were 152 workers that were eating up the investment budget. Mysteriously, in one year of administration, here was a bankrupt company, and I left 20 million bolivianos [surplus], and projects to execute the following year. So, it was a two-year plan. Stop corruption, restructure the company, prioritize projects and once the company was functioning at the end of 2010, I convene a public call to put someone in charge, someone elected for their ability, their knowledge. . . . That went against the interests of the mayor and I was dismissed. I was there for a year. The plan was not completed. . . .] There is an apparatus that is money. Efficiency in the system, that's the least of interest.
>
> (Former General Manager, Interview, 2014)

The "overstaffing" of Semapa is a point of contention among most people interviewed that work in the water sector (outside of the company) and citizens of Cochabamba. Many of these positions in Semapa are viewed as "favours." According to one former citizen representative, 70% of the 300 workers at Semapa worked in offices, doing little to contribute to the badly needed repairs to the water system (Former citizen representative, Interview, 2014). Accounts of corruption included inflating the quantity of materials necessary for a particular project and writing off equipment and supplies that never arrived. These repeated scandals diminished Semapa's chances for securing funding from international financial institutions that were already reluctant to invest in public companies (Sánchez Gómez & Terhorst, 2008). Once funds were invested, the instability of the company led to repeated cancellation of financing from the Inter-American Development Bank (Rodriguez, Interview, 2014).

Without vigorous social control to hold the company accountable to instances of corruption, the lack of strong participatory mechanisms was detrimental when projects did receive funding and reached the construction phase. One of the few major infrastructure projects that was successfully completed was the "Improvement of Potable Water System of Southeast Zone of Cochabamba City," commonly known as the JICA project, as it was funded by the Japanese International Cooperation Agency, which has operated in Bolivia for over three decades. The application for the project was first sent to JICA in 2004, and the project was completed in 2010. The goal was to provide water to 22 communities (OTBs) in the Southern Zone of Cochabamba, which would benefit an estimated 50,000 inhabitants, with the expansion of a water treatment facility, the construction of adduction and impulsion lines, the construction of a principal distribution network, and materials for secondary networks that would connect communities to the main network. Semapa would carry out the project with financial support from JICA. Construction faced its first obstacle when the community surrounding the treatment facility blocked its expansion because they did not want their neighbourhood disrupted. Semapa shifted course to the Aranjuez facility, where the water source would be. However, the inhabitants with usufruct rights did not permit Semapa to use the water, which lies outside its jurisdiction.

This lack of public participation and consultation resulted in the current state of the project: newly built infrastructure, but without water. When Evo Morales arrived to inaugurate the project (in October 2011), he opened the tap and water did flow freely, but without a regular water source the network is only working at 10% capacity, thereby accelerating pipe decay (Semapa worker, Interview, 2014). Rather than serving the neediest population of Cochabamba, the treatment facility improvements have benefited the residents of the Aranjuez district, one of the wealthiest neighbourhoods in the North of the city.

In 2011, some efforts were made to address corruption allegations and social commitments in Semapa, most noticeably with the establishment of the Transparency Unit, whose official mandate is to "[promote] the exercise of this instrument [of social control] by way of 'Public Accountability Hearings,' with the participation of citizens and social organization with respect to the interests and patrimony of the State" (Semapa, 2013, np). The objective of the unit is "transparency and the fight against corruption as a technical process to carry out actions aimed at making public management transparent; to prevent acts of corruption, to channel complaints on alleged corruption and/or lack of transparency of Semapa's civil servants" (Semapa, 2013, np). The Transparency Unit is housed within the branch of general management, responsible for ensuring that it remains transparent and tasked with developing the public participation mechanism through workshops and public discussions. The unit manager at the time was focused on 100% compliance with updating the information on Semapa's website. However, my repeated requests for formal directives or procedures for public participation and social control went unanswered.

Auditing corruption from within a company historically linked to internal corruption scandals may seem like a conflict of interest, but this is how Semapa proceeded. An example of this conflict was an instance of potential nepotism, where the director of Semapa's Planning Department awarded construction contracts to a company that he formerly owned but that was now registered under the name of his mother-in-law ("Semapa observada por adjudicaciones", 2014). "*Arjicons*" Aranivar Jaimes Engineering and Construction were granted at least nine work contracts from 2010–2014 valued at 4 million bolivianos. Competitors who claimed that their contracts were cancelled despite winning the bids brought complaints against Semapa. The Transparency Unit's investigation uncovered that the Director of Planning had only recently taken the role and had not authorized any projects to his relative's company. Half a year later, he was asked to declare his assets, suggesting some progress has been made on the corruption issue:

> Look, they have advanced. Perhaps not because of social control, but because of the new norms. Before, in Semapa, you could for example, purchase 100 containers of gas that Semapa didn't need, but nobody would say anything. Now, the new regulations state that you cannot spend outside of your Annual Operative Plan. You need to have an approved project in which to invest. So, there's a line of transparency that was not there before. Now it's more difficult to disburse an expense that doesn't exist. For example, how will Semapa justify 50 containers that aren't used?
>
> (Civil servant, Interview, 2014)

The Transparency Unit at least provides a space to bring allegations forward and provides a measure of control against unethical or corrupt practices. This kind of transparency certainly forms part of social control, yet remains within the old institutional framework.

Exclusionary practices emerge from participatory practices embedded within outdated or inadequate institutional frameworks, as evidenced within community-oriented projects. Again in 2011, the central government required Semapa to comply with participatory practices through the nationwide community development initiative known as DESCOM (*Desarrollo Comunitario y Fortalecimiento Institucional*—Community Development and Institutional Capacity Building), part of a requirement of most externally funded projects that need to meet the standards for the international Technical Economic Social and Environmental Assessment. In Semapa, DESCOM consists of hosting workshops with communities, water committees, and cooperatives on various water provision related topics, for example, tariffs or network maintenance. Externally hired consultants typically ran the workshops (Semapa worker, Interview, 2014). However, as one Semapa employee explained, little attention was paid to the social aspect of the assessment and projects. Often excluding community members from water projects, citizens did not learn how to use the service or receive training on network maintenance. Contracts for water provision between a community and Semapa would go unsigned, or Semapa would not receive payment for services, ultimately resulting in unused water systems:

> Years ago, they had [DESCOM] guides in many projects. But companies, even [Semapa] never gave much importance to the social part. They want it to work well technically, but forget that you need to work with people, that's when the problems start.
>
> (Semapa worker, Interview, 2014)

The national guides are based on previous DESCOM guides elaborated by the Inter-American Development Bank, which clearly state that the beneficiaries of the projects share "joint responsible" for project planning, execution, and evaluation (MMAyA, 2008). It is, however, difficult to determine the success of DESCOM beyond these guidelines and whether it fosters participation deeper than a consultation process. Semapa workers noted that DESCOM is even more complicated in a dense urban setting:

> We didn't have a person to do this work [of DESCOM]. So the engineers finally started the work and said "[the pipe] will pass here" and the people were opposed, there were blockades and strikes, they set fire to machinery, they sequestered the engineers for a full day. . . . Everything

was paralyzed, and the work did not start again until they explained it was the only option, the only way. In the end, the only way was to enter by force, with the police, with the mayor, with public force.

(Semapa worker, Interview, 2014)

This conflict in the Southern Zone, which occurred in late 2013, is not uncommon when Semapa enters a neighbourhood with no prior warning or explanation to install infrastructure that would serve a different neighbourhood. At other times, burst pipes or damaged sewage systems are left unattended for months. Throughout my interviews with members of water committees and cooperatives in the Southern Zone it was clear that collaboration and communication between the Cochabamba population and Semapa is badly wanting.

MAS and the rhetoric of social control

Optimism and expectations for improvements in the water and sanitation sector rose dramatically after the election of Evo Morales and the MAS government in 2005. The new government championed social control and participation in official discourse and policy while formalizing it in the water sector. In practice, however, MAS captured the idea of participation and social movements and reproduced clientelist relationships while access to higher-level decision-making remains restricted.

Morales ran on a platform of Indigenous rights, dignity, and sovereignty—a clear break from the colonial and racist regimes of the past. He also presented a shift from neoliberalism, predicated on the promise of nationalizing key industries and redistributing wealth through social programs for the most marginalized (Postero, 2010). A key principle of the MAS government is the Indigenous concept of *vivir bien*, or "good living," defined as "encounter and progress through diversity and 'inter-culturality,' harmony with nature, social and fraternal life, national sovereignty in all fields and internal accumulation with quality of life" (MMAyA, 2007). The concept is tied to Indigenous dignity and frames MAS's "Water for All" plan by arguing that water and access to water is fundamental to life, based on integrated water resources management that is sustainable and participatory (MMAyA, 2007).

MAS positioned themselves and projected themselves internationally as defenders of *Pachamama*, Mother Earth. Morales' successful lobbying efforts led to the ratification of United Nations Resolution (64/292) in July 2010 that expands the United Nations Declaration of Human Rights to recognize the Right to Water. The fundamental Right to Water was also an important part of the new Bolivian Constitution, putting the onus of guaranteeing access to water on the state and shifting ownership of water sources to public (read state) property, granting the "central level of state . . . exclusive authority over water resources" (Article 298, II). At the same time, the formal recognition of traditional and customary uses of water under Bolivian law and the creation of official licenses or registries for small-scale water providers became a large focus of water sector reform. The new potable water law (No. 2066) now created licenses for large providers such as municipalities (e.g. Semapa) and water committees, whether Indigenous communities, peasant unions, or neighbourhood associations, which would need to be registered as an EPSA (*Entidad prestador de sanamiento y agua*—water and sanitation provider). The changes in legislation were significant, as they signalled a shift in the dominant neoliberal model of water commercialization and provided protection against the threat of privatization (Boelens, 2008).

Another of Morales' first presidential acts was the creation of a national water authority. The Water Ministry encompassed vice-ministries responsible for policy, planning, and projects in the areas of potable water and basic sanitation, irrigation and water resources, environment and climate change [the current iteration is the Ministry of Environment and Water (MMAyA), under which fall the Vice Ministry of Potable Water and Basic Sanitation, the Vice Ministry of Water Resources and Irrigation, and the Vice Ministry of Environment, Biodiversity, Climate Change, and Forest Management and Development]. Notably, prominent figures in the anti-privatization water struggles were appointed as ministers and vice-ministers, including Luis Sánchez Gómez, appointed as Vice Minister of Basic Services in 2006, and Rene Orellana, appointed as Minister of Water in 2008. Through these types of appointments MAS could project its stance as a "party of social movements."

Under the umbrella of the Water Ministry, several corresponding agencies were established: the National Service for the Sustainability of Sanitation Services (SENASBA) to support community development, the Project-Executing Agency of Environment and Water (EMAGUA) to carry out water and sanitation projects, and the Fiscal and Social Control Authority (AAPS) and adjoining Technical Committee on Registrations and Licenses (a regulatory body for water service providers). AAPS is the entity responsible for creating a registry of the EPSAs in order to regulate water services. The process involves providing a registry or license that guarantees legal recognition to the EPSAs, offering jurisdictional security to the water service provider by registering the water source. The purported goal is to provide the EPSAs with protection against expropriation and operational support to strengthen the systems. Ideally, registering water sources and their uses helps avoid conflicts between communities and, importantly, creates a database of the existing water systems (AAPS Director, Interview, 2014). For the smaller, community-run EPSAs, registration came with the expectation of some form of benefits from the government.

The fate of Cochabamba's small-scale community-run systems or EPSAs presents a point of contention in the discussion of the potential expansion of Semapa's infrastructure (Bakker, 2010). Particularly, the registration of EPSAs calls attention to questions of jurisdiction and zones of responsibility in Cochabamba. The new legislation eliminated concession zones, and through registries and licenses granted small-scale systems jurisdiction over the water services in their zones, making them equal to Semapa before the law. This complicates planning and the expansion of Semapa into zones already serviced by smaller systems. Water committees and cooperatives in Cochabamba have engaged in a series of "multi-scalar strategies" to preserve their autonomy (Marston, 2014), yet many expressed apprehensions regarding the EPSA registration process. Indeed, in several interviews, people that worked within institutions reiterated that the sources did not actually belong to the communities, that the state was the regulator of water resources and their exploitation. An NGO worker in the water sector explained the different interpretations of the law that cause conflicts locally, citing an example in the nearby town of Vinto:

> In Vinto there are various water systems that have their wells, their structures, and they are independent from the municipality. Suddenly, one day, the Mayor decided to tell them they would be charged a tax. And if they want the [mayor's office] to perforate wells—because sometimes the municipality pays for well perforation in Vinto—one more well, the system will have to be transferred to the municipality. The law of autonomy establishes that municipalities have the responsibility, and can build infrastructure for water delivery systems. Moreover, it states that yes, they can, yes they must, they have money for infrastructure, wells, piping, whatever it may be.
>
> (Caneda, Interview, 2014)

Cases of parallel projects, competition between municipalities and communities over infrastructure and treatment facilities, are common in the Department of Cochabamba. Olivera (2014, Interview) criticizes the new legislation for diminishing the power of communities in a process that favours the state: "those who seek access to water are increasingly forced to go to the state, the laws, the courts." Where disputes were previously settled between communities through uses and customs, several state agencies are now set to intervene. Further, Seeman (2016) faults the legislation for idealizing community harmony. Echoing Perreault's (2008) argument, Seeman (2016) acknowledges that inclusive water governance can be beneficial for communal water rights. However, rather than levelling the playing field, participating in the liberal justice system excludes communities unable to record their water consumption through uses and customs: "formal recognition of local hydrosocial territories necessarily implies the non-recognition and illegalization of a variety of non-formalized hydrosocial territories" (Seeman, 2016, p. 169), concluding that MAS's approach is a form of "disciplinary water governance," as the formalization of the water sector can obscure inequalities in access to resources.

The potential for registries and licenses to heighten inequality must be evaluated against the material impact of EPSA recognition. As of 2014, according to information provided by AAPS, 46 EPSAs had registered in Cochabamba. Many water committees expressed frustrations over the minimal assistance received—obtaining formal recognition had not changed much. Without regulation over drilling wells or analysis of water samples, AAPS functions as an outlet for complaints or conflicts that are not resolved within communities. This returns to Olivera's point that the formalization of the water sector has created a certain dependence on the state. A change in interactions with the state is observed in the way social movements and communities increasingly place demands upon MAS rather than seek their own solutions or alternatives, as had been done previously.

The policies and projects under the Water for All campaign seek to prioritize districts that lack access to water, with a heavy focus on rural areas and irrigation programs. The Vice Minister of Water (at the time) proclaimed that water access for 99% of Bolivians would be achieved by 2020 (Vice Minister of Water, Interview, 2014). However, the actual figures are more modest: 80.8% have water access nationally, and in Cochabamba the figures are 68.7% for water and 54% for basic sanitation (INE, 2014). Of the basic sanitation number, 54.6% consists of piped sewage systems, while 45.4% consists of alternatives such as septic tanks and cesspits (INE, 2014). Further, the national statistics can be misleading because they focus on infrastructure, ignoring other criteria of quality, quantity, and continuity of services (Campanini, 2014). The national government projects focused on water and sanitation have had mixed outcomes.

One of the largest projects under the Water for All campaign is *Mi Agua* (My Water). Several reports outline subpar construction of *Mi Agua* projects that were hastily executed to demonstrate results in order to garner favour with voters or reward support:

In the period of elections, they distributed cheques for *Mi Agua* in a first phase. So in one [area] that already had a [water] system, they gifted a cheque intended for two [communities], to destroy the system and rebuild another one. So it's disruptive when it could have been used in a place that is in need. This is done to bring them on your side. On the other hand, I was working on DESCOM for three *Mi Agua* projects, a package that was between La Paz, Cochabamba, and Santa Cruz, three sewage systems. What I saw is that the systems were there because the communities had been supportive of the government. In other words, they had been given as a reward.

(NGO worker, Interview, 2014)

This kind of exchange is not unique to the MAS government. In her book *El Alto, Rebel City*, Lazar (2007) depicts the historical norms of patronage politics in Bolivia; what is distinct in the MAS regime is the position the party takes as the voice of social movements. The critique levelled from the left charges Morales of co-opting the movements. As Regalsky explains (2010, p. 47), the push for political reform and Indigenous recognition in fact "subordinated [groups] to the state" and reinforced the party system, thereby demobilizing the movements due to loss of leadership and neutralizing the critical lens (Regalsky, Interview, 2014). Hierarchical clientelist relations between the political party and voters are reproduced yet are more obscured under the MAS government. This limits social movements' abilities to work beyond the frameworks proposed by MAS.

In the water sector, this dynamic has led groups to align themselves with MAS's position specifically to gain funding. The most notable example in the Cochabamba context is ASICA-SUDD-EPSAS's wavering position regarding the autonomy of water committees. ASICA-SUDD-EPSAS is the umbrella organization representing many small-scale water systems of the Southern Zone. At its inception in 2004, the organization's stance was a defence of these water systems against dispossession by foreign capital. ASICA-SUDD-EPSAS was open to working jointly with Semapa on the administration of water and sanitation services, yet was steadfast about maintaining their autonomy (Grandydier & Tinta, 2006). Influenced by the political climate, today the organization's position has shifted to align with the conception of EPSAs existing within an overarching municipal system, viewing the small-scale systems as unsustainable. ASICA-SUDD-EPSAS's perspective no longer fully upholds community management as a real alternative:

What I saw was a problem with the organizational capacity in the association. Many that call themselves social organizations in Bolivia have encountered this problem. The relationship with the government is very complicated. In the sense that an autonomous organization perhaps takes a critical position and loses access to spaces of negotiation, funding, etc. Meanwhile, an organization that is more in tune with the government gains many advantages, but perhaps loses its autonomy and organizational capacity, capacity for collective action, that is decision-making, having autonomous positions. I think that ASICA[-SUDD-EPSAS] entered into this dynamic. By ingratiating themselves with the government, they lost a bit of autonomy, spontaneity, credibility amongst their partners, and finally, strength as an association. So I think on one hand this happened, the leaders diluted the strength and autonomy of ASICA[-SUDD-EPSAS] to be more aligned with the governmental apparatus, just like what happened to many social organizations.

(NGO worker, Interview, 2014)

Being less critical of MAS was a tactic to gain technical or financial assistance to help maintain the systems at the cost of the association's ability to organize independently from the state. Paradoxically, any benefits received from aligning with MAS have not translated to advantages for the water committees of the Southern Zone. Instead, the organization is fragmented and no longer presents a strong unified front. ASICA-SUDD-EPSAS has weakened substantially, especially since the loss of funding from international donors.

Once numerous in the Cochabamba Valley, the presence of internationally-funded NGOs also appears to be on the wane. Since the controversy surrounding TIPNIS,[5] there is an increasingly contentious relationship between MAS and NGOs critical of the government's extractivist policies that contradict their position as champions for the environment and Indigenous populations (Achtenberg, 2015). In May 2015, Morales issued Decree 2366, opening natural protected areas to mining and oil extraction. A month later, the President threatened to expel "imperialist" NGOs that challenged the decree (Ruiz, 2015).[6] However, as Spronk (2014) points out, the basic funding structure for the water and sanitation sector in Bolivia is unchanged since the neoliberal era, reliant on external funding from international cooperation. The Minister of Finance reported 8.417 million bolivianos assigned to water and sanitation projects since 2006, when MAS took office nationally ("Gobierno asegura que desde 2006 invirtió Bs 8.427 millones en proyectos de agua", 2016). This figure is not a sizable investment when compared to the climbing GDP (from USD 11.542 billion in 2006 to USD 32.998 billion in 2016) due to the rise in commodities exports. Public spending is devoted to more visible and popular construction projects, for example, bridges, paving roads, plazas, and soccer fields. For many in Cochabamba, this means large water and sewage infrastructure projects remain dependent upon external donors and their conditionalities. But for the water committees and cooperatives in the Southern Zone facing financial constraints, there is less direct support from international cooperation and greater reliance on funding allocated through government institutions, while the crisis of unequal access to water persists.

Lasting neoliberal logic

Despite the abolition of the private contract and the strong anti-privatization sentiment that followed the Water War, water commodification is still present in Bolivia today, further undermining the establishment of a strong public participatory alternative. Nickson and Vargas (2002) argued that privatization could have extended the municipal system to poorer neighbourhoods had there been more time to develop, and a number of people working in the water sector echo these claims. They do not categorically reject the involvement of the private sector in water services and continue to consider the possibility of a public–private system today. In fact, while the Constitution outlines that the State is responsible for guaranteeing access to water, it does make reference to mixed water providers, which could include a private profit-seeking component (Spronk, 2014). Free market ideology is difficult to extinguish. The ongoing existence of private sellers of water in Cochabamba underscores the argument that the shift to post-neoliberalism is not categorical (Webber, 2011). Private water sales are a product of the weaknesses of Cochabamba's public system, but they also provide a crutch for inaction on the part of government.

In Cochabamba, the most concrete illustration of this water commercialization tension can be found in the bottled water industry, mainly serving the Northern and Central Zones of the city. The wealthier population and most restaurants use bottled water for drinking and cooking as a supplement to municipal Semapa water for reasons of unreliable service and poor quality. There are 34 authorized bottled water companies in Cochabamba, regulated by the Departmental Health Services through quality analysis. The industry is reluctant to release information on distribution and water sources, but in 2015 there was a reported increase in water bottle companies amidst the water shortages in the area. This forms part of a growing global bottled water industry thriving on urban water insecurity (Pacheco-Vega, 2019).

Many EPSAs source their water from their own community wells, but sometimes must rely on cistern water which is sourced from private wells of homeowners sitting on groundwater located in the Northern Zone of the city. These homeowners sell to the *aguateros*, who collect the water in trucks and distribute largely to neighbourhoods that do not have access to the Semapa networks. The *aguateros'* business comprises the other important unregulated private water sales in Cochabamba. The *aguateros* joined the fight against privatization, though likely for more self-interested reasons; they too would lose business, as the wells they depend upon fell into Aguas del Tunari's concession zone. After the Water War, the *aguateros* resumed their water delivery service, though today this practice technically contravenes the new Constitution. For years, government officials have turned a blind eye to this practice, based on the argument that without the *aguateros*, the most marginalized segment of the population would be denied water. As the sector is unregulated, there is little public knowledge of the water quality or the use of groundwater.

At the height of the drought in the winter of 2016, it was not uncommon to observe run-off water from private cisterns streaming down the streets in the Northern Zone. Moreover, there is no control over the pricing of this water or the delivery routes. The irony is, of course, that the *aguateros* mostly render services to the people who drove the fight against privatization. Opponents of privatization are obliged to partake in a system of commercialized water without having a say in how it functions. They are also put into a precarious position, at the mercy of the *aguateros*, because they are often their only source of water. During the drought, the *aguateros* sold water at increasingly higher rates based on the principles of market demand. They also began delivering water to the Central Zones of Cochabamba, whose residents had their water rationed by Semapa. For the *aguateros*, diverting water from the lower-income Southern Zone communities meant they could charge higher rates and travel less.

In 2016, as a response to the drought crisis, the regional AAPS agency attempted to regulate the sector by calling meetings with actors in the water sector. Municipal and departmental government officials were noticeably absent from these meetings. *Aguateros* were present, but as they were not interested in regulating the price of water, they did not attend subsequent meetings. During the first session, a representative from the *aguateros* union explained that they work according to demand and justified the price spike due to increased demand, distance travelled, and off-season dips in demand (Fieldwork observation, 2016). To their credit, driving cistern trucks can be classified as precarious work given the long waits to fill the tanks, the long hours driving on difficult terrain in old trucks that are generally not in great condition, and the uncertainty of work in the off-season rainy months. It is difficult to obtain first-hand accounts of *aguateros*' work, however, as they are very cautious about exposing themselves; in the current climate they feel vilified in the media. *Aguateros* defend their business and characterize the work as a public service to the people of Cochabamba. Yet they are not delivering water out of civic duty; it remains a commercial transaction and one that excludes public input.

The *aguateros*' aversion to regulation also stems from experiences of inconsistency when dealing with state institutions. The most repeated example is the mechanism of obtaining a yearly stamp on a cistern from the Departmental Health Services as a sign of quality assurance. The *aguateros* lamented the out-of-pocket cost and the lack of diligence in verification, which deterred them from continuing the process. The well owners themselves claimed to be more open about collaborating with AAPS. They justified the sale of water to the *aguateros* at 40 bolivianos a tank as a small and defensible recuperation of the initial investment of well construction and the costs of operations, though these costs are not transparent. The well owners affirmed they would shut down operations once Semapa had the ability to provide water to all citizens and once the Misicuni project was functioning, with the latter having a conveniently undetermined and ever-changing deadline.

The dilemma of the *aguateros* challenges the argument often made by the municipality that water demands cannot be met due to water scarcity in the Cochabamba Valley. Rather, it points to the ineffective management and distribution of the resource. Dependence on this "band-aid" solution feeds the complacency of the municipal government and Semapa. As long as private water delivery is responding to needs, there is less urgency for the government to act.

Transformative participation in the city: *Maria Auxiliadora* community

To reach Maria Auxiliadora from Cochabamba's bus terminal, a forty-minute *trufi* ride weaves through the city's Southern Zone, and paved roads give way to dirt paths en route to District 9, Sivingani. The Maria Auxiliadora community—Habitat for Women (*Hábitat para la mujer—Comunidad Maria Auxiliadora*) is an example of transformative participation on the peri-urban fringe of the city. Whereas the remunicipalization of Semapa failed to build transformative participatory practices, the Maria Auxiliadora community embodies a space of inclusive governance and participatory decision-making, empowering women to organize around their needs. Nevertheless, water remains a site of struggle and resistance as the community continues to face external pressures (Mohanty & Miraglia, 2012).

Maria Auxiliadora was founded on 21 September 1999, a few years after a Women's Network and Housing conference (*Red Mujer y Hábitat*) in 1996 where the association of women neighbourhood leaders (*Asociación de Mujeres Lideres Bariales*) made the link between domestic violence and the right to housing. In Bolivia, the high rate of femicide resulting from domestic violence is tied to housing insecurity. Women facing domestic abuse generally have few options: prejudice in the rental system and an inadequate government housing program maintain women in a vulnerable position for fear of losing housing. The *mujeres lideres* resolved to address violence against women and housing insecurity by creating an alternative community based on the principles of collective living. Identifying the housing crisis for single mothers and survivors of sexual and domestic violence, the women resolved to found a community to provide dignified housing (*vivienda digna*) through an alternative community of collective property, female leadership, family-oriented community, and participation (APA, 2014, p. 11).

To facilitate housing for low-income families and single mothers, the alternative property regime offers a 200 m² lot for USD 600 that can be paid over time; a relatively low sum when comparable plots in the area are sold for upwards of USD 9,000 (Periferia, 2014). Purchases do not provide private property titles; rather, the families agree to join the community and the property remains collective (*colectiva comunitaria*). As one of the community founders, RoseMary Irustra, explains, the collective housing system ensures guaranteed housing and protection for women and children. A common problem in Cochabamba is that when the spouse leaves and/or sells the family house, the mother and children are left homeless. In the Maria Auxiliadora community, the house cannot be sold. This collective property model, more common in rural regions, is unique to Cochabamba's urban periphery.

The participation model in the community is not unlike other neighbourhood associations in the Southern Zone of Cochabamba; decisions are reached during mandatory monthly assemblies; members participate in community work, community labour, and contributions for community building projects; Andean traditions like *kermes* and *pasanaku* reinforce Andean principles of solidarity and reciprocity. The distinction in Maria Auxiliadora that embodies transformative participation is the collective property arrangement and the participatory space created for marginalized women. The community is women-centric; of the first 450 families that joined the community, all but 15 were headed by women (Periferia, 2014, p. 170). Female leadership is a key pillar of the community, as the neighbourhood association charter requires the President and Vice-Present to be female. The community neighbourhood watch formed support committees for domestic abuse and established strict policy against abusers. Assemblies are punctuated by anti-violence seminars. Moreover, the community prohibits the sale of alcohol. Through the Network of Women Neighbourhood Leaders, community members also participated in the constituent assembly process across the country in 2006, which achieved the inclusion of Article 19, "Right to Shelter," in the new Constitution (APA, 2014, p. 4).

Similar to many peri-urban settlements of the Southern Zone, Maria Auxiliadora does not have access to the municipal water service, Semapa. Like many other communities, Maria Auxiliadora was able to build potable water and sewage systems through community work and self-financing and support from the NGO sector and international cooperation. Major financing came from Pro-Habitat Foundation credits as well as support from CIPRO-DEC (Swiss cooperation), UNITAS, and Fundación Aguatuya (APA, 2014, p. 4). As the community did not have OTB status for several years due to bureaucratic delays, they did not receive any funding through the Law of Popular Participation (Unzueta Pérez, 2012). In a region often ignored by the state, the community administered their own funds to improve the system, with monthly contributions from members. The water system is self-sustained via monthly tariffs, but major improvements have been financed through NGO funding (APA, 2014, p. 9). The community's women-centric ethos was attractive for funders. The community built their water system thanks to a grant with CIPRODEC Swiss cooperation. Pro-Habitat funded the sewage system, while the community contributed the labour. By 2004, they had a well that provided water at the rate of 3 L/s.

The community was thriving and expanding; however, in 2011, confrontations within the community began. Influenced by land speculators (*lote-adores*) and profits made in surrounding neighbourhoods, a faction of the community decided they wanted to "reclaim" the individual titles of their land in order to sell their homes (Periferia, 2014, p. 11). Thus began a rift between those who wanted to maintain the collective spirit of the community and those seeking private ownership. The water system became the site of conflict and escalating violence. The dissenting group withheld payments and contributions, destroyed the water pump, leaving the community without water, and sabotaged community work on an 80-m trench (which caused the project funders to pull out). Threats escalated to legal action: the dissenting group demanded land titles under Law 247 Urban Property Regularization ("Activistas piden liberar a Irusta", 2012) and accused community founder, RoseMary Irusta, of fraud, as the land purchased remained in her name. Irusta spent four months in a women's detention centre awaiting trial.

The group trying to obtain land titles had ties to property developers and the mayor's office (Community Member, Interview 2016). Both groups were vying for legal recognition. One side was trying to obtain recognition as a collective under the Constitutional Right to Collective-Community Property, though this is only recognized in rural zones. The other side submitted for legal recognition as a neighbourhood committee (*junta vecinal*) with individual property titles. The first group's application was denied, just as the deputy mayor of the Southern Zone began to threaten to demolish houses in the community ("Activistas piden liberar a Irusta", 2012). Meanwhile, the Mayor of Cercado approved the minority group's legal status, ignoring complaints from the original Maria Auxiliadora community of violence resulting from the conflict.

The court case against Irusta was eventually dismissed, and she was released. However, the community remains fractioned and faces uncertainty. The Maria Auxiliadora community faces difficulties in obtaining collective land status from the municipality because the community does not correspond to a traditional Indigenous community. The underlying issue is that the alternative property regime presents a threat to the local elites.

The community continues to receive threats from surrounding landlords, and the governance of the water system is unresolved. The case presents the structural barriers to transformative participation and a further example of how MAS's rhetoric of social control and participation fails to translate to protection for marginalized members of society.

Conclusion

In Cochabamba, the remunicipalization of water services falls far short of the more successful experience of other cities around the world (Kishimoto & Petitjean, 2017). Rather, it is associated with a system of elite capture, clientelism, and corruption. The demands from the Water War were not reached, in part due to the tensions around defining participation and public. This chapter has unpacked the different challenges to building a strong public alternative that includes participation and social control. Transformative participation and practices of social control exist within the Cochabamba water sector, as in the case of Maria Auxiliadora, but have failed to concretize at the municipal water service provider Semapa. The current mechanism of participation in Semapa resembles a public relations exercise intended to gain legitimacy. MAS and Evo Morales have instituted several changes in the water and sanitation sector at the national level, but these, too, have not resulted in the changes hoped for. The language utilized throughout legal and policy documents upholds public participation in governance and can be interpreted on the surface as transformative, but public participation is contained in state-sanctioned spaces with little facilitation of participation in higher-level decision-making. Only organizations and social movements that are not perceived as a threat to MAS are invited to take part.

The formalization of the public water sector has not resulted in much material change either. The newer institutions are associated with bureaucratic ineffectiveness due to the constant rotation of Ministers and the duplication of responsibilities across departments. More broadly, there have not yet been any updates to the century-old General Water Law that dates to 1906, resulting in competition for the multiple uses of water across sectors. The new Constitution protects the Human Right to Water, but in practice MAS does not prioritize residential water issues. Consequently, Cochabamba continues to face an increasingly severe water crisis.

Notes

1 Bolivian companies ICE A.I.E., SoBACE, C.B.I., and CoPesa each held 5% shares (de Gramont, 2006, p. 10).
2 All interview quotes are translated from Spanish by the author.

3 Lazar (2007) and other scholars on Andean identity identify the transience of Indigenous identity, often used in strategic ways to navigate different spaces.
4 A spike in attendance occurred in 2016 due to the drastic drought situation.
5 The Trans-Oceanic Highway, a joint infrastructure mega-project between Bolivia, Brazil, and Peru, consists of a large-scale highway across the Isiboro Sécure National Park TIPNIS (*Territorio Indígena y Parque Nacional Isiboro Sécure*), affecting over sixty Indigenous communities. NGOs highly critical of the road for its environmental impact on the Amazonian rainforest and the displacement of Indigenous communities were reproached and threatened by MAS and in one case expelled from the country. See McNeish (2013) and Achtenburg (2015) for further reading.
6 International NGOs or foundations are not the only targets, however. Most recently the Centre for Information and Documentation of the University of San Simon, the largest archives and research centre in Cochabamba, is being displaced from their offices for their criticism of MAS's natural resource exploitation.

References

Achtenberg, E. (2015). Morales greenlights TIPNIS road, oil and gas extraction in Bolivia's National Parks. *NACLA Rebel Currents*. http://blog/2015/06/15/morales-greenlights-tipnis-road-oil-and-gas-extraction-bolivia%E2%80%99s-national-parks

Activistas piden liberar a Irusta, Cochabamba. (2012). *Los Tiempos*.

Aguilar Miranda, L. A., & Miranda Hernández, M. A. (2012). La participación política: Entre la concesión institucional y la conquista popular. In M. A. Gandarillas (Ed.), *Democracia participativa: ¿Realidad o espejismo?* (pp. 7–33). CEDIB.

Ahlers, R. (2005). Empowering or disempowering: The gender dimensions of neoliberal water policy in Mexico and Bolivia. In V. Bennett, S. Dávila-Poblete, & M. N. Rico (Eds.), *Opposing currents: The politics of water and gender in Latin America* (pp. 53–71). University of Pittsburgh Press. www.jstor.org/stable/j.ctt9qh61c

American Planning Association (APA). (2014). *Hábitat para la mujer Comunidad Maria Auxiliadora*. APA.

Assies, W. (2003). David versus Goliath in Cochabamba. *Latin American Perspectives*, *30*(3), 14–36. https://doi.org/10.1177/0094582X03030003003

Bakker, K. J. (2010). *Privatizing water: Governance failure and the world's urban water crisis*. Cornell University Press.

Barja Daza, G., & Urquiola, M. (2005). Bolivian capitalization and privatization: Approximation to an evaluation. In J. R. Nellis & N. Birdsall (Eds.), *Reality check: The distributional impact of privatization in developing countries* (pp. 123–177). Center for Global Development.

Bennett, V. (1995). *The politics of water: Urban protest, gender, and power in Monterrey, Mexico*. University of Pittsburgh Press.

Boelens, R. (2008). Water rights arenas in the Andes: Upscaling networks to strengthen local water control. *Water Alternatives*, *1*(1), 48–65.

Budds, J., & McGranahan, G. (2003). Are the debates on water privatization missing the point? Experiences from Africa, Asia and Latin America. *Environment & Urbanization*, *15*(2), 87–114. https://doi.org/10.1177/095624780301500222

Bustamante, R., & Gutiérrez, Z. (1999). Usos y costumbres en la gestion de riego: Caos u orden en la gestión de agua para riego. In P. Hoogendam (Ed.), *Aguas y municipios: Retos para la gestión municipal de agua para riego* (pp. 163–188). PEIRAV, Plural Editores.

Bustamante, R., Peredo, E., & Udaeta, M. E. (2005). Women in the "water war" in the Cochabamba Valleys. In V. Bennett, S. Dávila-Poblete, & M. N. Rico (Eds.), *Opposing currents: The politics of water and gender in Latin America*. University of Pittsburgh Press. www.jstor.org/stable/j.ctt9qh61c

Campanini, O. (2014). Agua y saneamiento: Elementos de análisis de la actual política (Parte I). *Petropress, 33*, 48–56.

Cleaver, F. (2001). Institutions, agency, and the limitation of participatory approaches to development. In B. Cooke & U. Kothari (Eds.), *Participation: The new tyranny?* Zed Books.

Conaghan, C. M., & Malloy, J. M. (1994). *Unsettling statecraft: Democracy and neoliberalism in the central Andes*. University of Pittsburgh Press.

Coordinadora de Defensa del Agua y Vida (Coordinadora). (2001). *SEMAPA con control social: Propuesta de estatutos para el manejo de la empresa*. Coordinadora.

Crespo, C. F. (1999). *La guerra de los pozos*. CERES.

Crespo, C. F. (2006). *La ley de riego y sus reglamentos: Riesgos y desafíos: Vol. Boletín 78*. Comisión para la Gestión Integral del Agua en Bolivia (CGIAB).

Crespo, C. F., & Fernández, O. (2004). *Estado, movimientos sociales y recursos hidricos. Presión social y negociación luego de la guerra del agua de Cochabamba*. CESU-UMSS.

Crespo, C. F., Peredo, C., & Omar, F. (2004). *Los regantes de Cochabamba en la guerra del agua: Presión social y negociación*. CESU-UMSS.

Dangl, B. (2007). *The price of fire: Resource wars and social movements in Bolivia*. AK Press.

de Gramont, A. (2006). After the Water War: The Battle for Jurisdiction in Aguas Del Tunari, S.A. v. Republic of Bolivia. Transnational Dispute Management (TDM) 3.

Driessen, T. (2008). Collective management strategies and elite resistance in Cochabamba, Bolivia. *Development, 51*, 89–95.

Estado Plurinacional de Bolivia (EPB). (2009). *Nueva constitución política del estado*. UPS, LaPaz.

Garande, T., & Dagg, S. (2005). Public participation and effective water governance at the local level: A case study from a small under-developed area in Chile. *Environment, Development and Sustainability, 7*(4), 417–431. https://doi.org/10.1007/s10668-004-3323-9

Gobierno asegura que desde 2006 invirtió Bs 8.417 millones en proyectos de agua, Cochabamba. (2016). *Los Tiempos*.

Goldman, M. (2007). How "water for all!" policy became hegemonic: The power of the World Bank and its transnational policy networks. *Geoforum, 38*(5), 786–800. https://doi.org/10.1016/j.geoforum.2005.10.008

Grandydier, F., & Tinta, R. (2006). Experiencia de la asociación de sistemas comunitarios de agua potbale de la zona Sur del municipio de Cochabamba. In F. Quiroz, N. Faysse, & R. Ampuero (Eds.), *Apoyo a la gestión de comités de agua* potable: Experiencias de fortalecimiento a comités de agua potable comunitarios en Bolivia y Colombia* (pp. 239–258). Centro AGUA-UMSS.

INE (Instituto Nacional de Estadísticas), Estado Plurinacional de Bolivia. (2014). Censo Nacional de Población y Vivienda. *Statistics.* www.ine.gov.bo

Kishimoto, S., & Petitjean, O. (Eds.). (2017). *Reclaiming public services: How cities and citizens are turning back privatisation.* Transnational Institute.

Laurie, N. (2011). Gender water networks: Femininity and masculinity in water politics in Bolivia. *International Journal of Urban and Regional Research, 35*(1), 172–188. https://doi.org/10.1111/j.1468-2427.2010.00962.x

Lazar, S. (2007). *El Alto, Rebel City: Self and citizenship in Andean Bolivia* (W. D. Mignolo, I. Silverblatt, & S. Saldívar-Hull, Eds.). Duke University Press. https://doi.org/10.1215/9780822388760

Marston, A. J. (2014). The scale of informality: Community-run water systems in peri-urban Cochabamba, Bolivia. *Water Alternatives, 7*, 72–88.

McNeish, J.-A. (2013). Extraction, protest and indigeneity in Bolivia: The TIPNIS effect. *Latin American and Caribbean Ethnic Studies, 8*(2), 221–242. https://doi.org/10.1080/17442222.2013.808495

Michener, V. J. (1998). The participatory approach: Contradiction and co-option in Burkina Faso. *World Development, 26*(12), 2105–2118. https://doi.org/10.1016/S0305-750X(98)00112-0

MMAyA. (2007). *Plan nacional de desarollo del riego para "Vivir Bien": 2007–2011.* Ministerio del Agua, Viceministerio de Riego.

MMAyA. (2008). *Guía de desarollo comunitario en proyecto de agua y saniamiento.* Ministerio del Agua, Viceministerio de Riego.

Mohanty, C. T., & Miraglia, S. (2012). Gendering justice, building alternative futures. In D. A. McDonald & G. Ruiters (Eds.), *Alternatives to privatization: Public options for essential services in the Global South* (pp. 71–98). HSRC Press.

Narain, S. (2006). Community-led alternatives to water management: India case study. *Human Development Report Occasional Paper.* http://hdr.undp.org/en/content/community-led-alternatives-water-management-india-case-study

Nickson, A., & Vargas, C. (2002). The limitations of water regulation: The failure of the Cochabamba Concession in Bolivia. *Bulletin of Latin American Research, 21*(1), 99–120.

Olivera, O., & Lewis, T. (2004). *¡Cochabamba!: Water war in Bolivia.* South End Press.

Pacheco-Vega, R. (2019). (Re)theorizing the politics of bottled water: Water insecurity in the context of weak regulatory regimes. *Water, 11*(4), 658. https://doi.org/10.3390/w11040658

Periferia. (2014). *Buscar un lugar . . . Y construir una comunidad "Hoy por ti y mañana por mí," Comunidad María Auxiliadora, Cochabamba.* Miserear.

Perreault, T. (2008). Custom and contradiction: Rural water governance and the politics of Usos y Costumbres in Bolivia's irrigators' movement. *Annals of the Association of American Geographers, 98*(4), 834–854. https://doi.org/10.1080/00045600802013502

Postero, N. (2010). Morales's MAS government. *Latin American Perspectives, 37*(3), 18–34. https://doi.org/10.1177/0094582X10364031

Regalsky, P. (2010). Political processes and the reconfiguration of the state in Bolivia. *Latin American Perspectives*, *37*(3), 35–50.

Ruiz, C. (2015). Bolivian vice president García Linera vs. NGOs: A look at the debate. *Upside Down World*. http://upsidedownworld.org/archives/bolivia/bolivian-vice-president-garcia-linera-vs-ngos-a-look-at-the-debate/

Sánchez Gómez, L., & Terhorst, P. (2005). Cochabamba, Bolivia: Public-collective partnerships after the water war. In Balanya, Brennan, Hoedeman, Kishimoto, & P. Terhorst (Eds.), *Reclaiming public water: Achievements, struggles, and visions from around the world* (pp. 121–130). TNI.

Seemann, M. (2016). Inclusive recognition politics and the struggle over hydrosocial territories in two Bolivian highland communities. *Water International*, *41*(1), 157–172.

Semapa observada por adjudicaciones, Cochabamba. (2014). *Los Tiempos*.

Semapa. (2013). *Programa operativo annual: Gestión 2013*. Semapa.

Shiva, V. (2002). *Water wars: Privatization, pollution, and profit*. Pluto.

Shultz, J. (2008). The Cochabamba water revolt and its aftermath. In M. C. Draper & J. Shultz (Eds.), *Dignity and defiance: Stories from Bolivia's challenge to globalization* (pp. 9–43). University of California Press.

Spronk, S. (2007). Roots of resistance to urban water privatization in Bolivia: The "new working class," the crisis of neoliberalism, and public services. *International Labor and Working-Class History*, *71*(1), 8–28. https://doi.org/10.1017/S0147547907000312

Spronk, S. (2009). Water privatization and the prospects for trade union revitalization in the public sector: Case studies from Bolivia and Peru. *Just Labour: A Canadian Journal of Work and Society*, *14*, 164–176.

Spronk, S. (2014). *Post-neoliberalism in Latin America? Urban water supply management in Bolivia under Evo Morales*. Putting Public in Public Services: Research, Action and Equity in the Global South.

Spronk, S., & Crespo, C. F. (2008). Water, national sovereignty and social resistance: Bilateral investment treaties and the struggles against multinational water companies in Cochabamba and El Alto, Bolivia. *Law, Social Justice & Global Development Journal (LGD)*, *1*.

Unzueta Pérez, W. (2012). En el D-9 termina una década de postergación para 13 OTB's. *Gente*.

Wainwright, H. (2012). Transformative resistance: The role of labour and trade unions in alternatives to privatization. In D. A. McDonald & G. Ruiters (Eds.), *Alternatives to privatization: Public options for essential services in the Global South* (pp. 71–98). HSRC Press.

Webber, J. R. (2011). *From rebellion to reform in Bolivia: Class struggle, indigenous liberation, and the politics of Evo Morales*. Haymarket Books.

5 Participatory mechanisms beyond Semapa

The previous chapter established the largely nominal experience of participation and social control in the context of an unsteady remunicipalization of Cochabamba's formal water provider, Semapa. This chapter extends the analysis by applying these analytical frameworks to broader water governance initiatives in the city, specifically, the Misicuni Multipurpose Project, a dam scheme built to deliver bulk water to Cochabamba, and a comparison of the Metropolitan Master Plan and the Water Agenda, two competing initiatives for future water governance. Once again, the focus is on how public participation has been envisioned and implemented in these water initiatives, offering further insight into the deep-seated tensions around the meaning and practice of public participation and how it affects the ability of Cochabambinos to create transformative social control in the water and sanitation sector in the future.

Misicuni lies at the heart of the long-term strategy to manage Cochabamba's water crisis. Dating back to the 1950s, the dam project is grounded in a modernist solution to urban water delivery and has been riddled with delays and accounts of corruption since its inception. Nevertheless, it remains central to the more recent Metropolitan Master Plan, commissioned by the Bolivian Water Ministry. Both Misicuni and the Metropolitan Master Plan are lacking when it comes to participatory mechanisms, however, a shortcoming that an alternative water governance strategy— the Water Agenda—attempts to address, suggesting spaces where it might be possible to recuperate a more transformative form of participation and social control.

Pipe dreams: The Misicuni Multipurpose Project

The potential of Misicuni River as a main source of water for the Cochabamba Valley was first explored by engineer Luis Calvo Soux in 1957 (Vera Varela, 1995), over a decade prior to the formation of the municipal

DOI: 10.4324/9781003169383-5

water company Semapa. Thereafter, the Misicuni Multipurpose Project has formed the longstanding proposal to bring water to the Cochabamba Valley in the collective consciousness of Cochabambinos; see Table 5.1 for a timeline of the Misicuni project (Vera Varela, 1995; Laurie & Marvin, 1999). Across my interviews, people lamented the project's perpetual postponements and redesigns and its association with technical flaws and a myriad of corruption scandals, fuelling citizens' mistrust of the Bolivian state. However sceptical though, the majority of interviewees maintained that Misicuni was important for meeting Cochabamba's water needs.

Table 5.1 Timeline of the Misicuni Multipurpose Project

Dates	Phase of Misicuni project
1957	Engineer Luis Calvo Soux identifies Misicuni as a potential water source.
1970s	First studies conducted on the feasibility of Misicuni.
1978–9	Feasibility study carried out by consortium Valois-Galindo determined initial construction steps of building a 120-m dam and a 19.5-km tunnel.
1992	Construction begins but incurs financial and legal problems that lead to delays.
1995	The "Ventana de Calio" is built with financing from Italian cooperation.
1997–2006	First phase of the Misicuni Multipurpose Project Construction begins on the 19.5-km tunnel with a USD 80 million investment. Work on the tunnel culminates after 96 months (original estimate of 42 months); carries a minimal amount of water to Cochabamba.
2006	Bidding begins on the construction of the dam and related projects. Further delays prevent the construction that was set to begin in 2007.
2009	Second phase of the Misicuni Multipurpose Project Agreement reached and signed in 2009 for dam construction (USD 84 million) to culminate in 2013. However, the contract ended with Consocio Hidroeletrico Misicuni (in 2013) due to mismanagement of funds.
2014	The Misicuni project is reinitiated under Supreme Decree 1946. CAMCE is granted the contract.
2016	Dam structure is concluded; capacity to collect 180 million cubic metres of water. Third phase of Misicuni project in the design stage: to construct a second tunnel to the Putucni and Visachas rivers.
2017	Misicuni supplies water to the city of Cochabamba, though it does not reach all of the population; problems with the irrigation component of the project.
2021	MMAyA signs a contract with Misicuni company to construct a 15-km adduction to deliver water to the Southern Zone of Cochabamba, with a USD 290,700 investment.

In short, the project consists of diverting the Misicuni, Viscachas, and Putucuni rivers, located in the mountain range to the north of the city, towards Cochabamba. The main construction comprises of a 120-m-high dam in Angosto de Sivingani on the Misicuni River, and a 19.5-km tunnel, with smaller dams to capture water from Visacachas and Putucuni and tunnels to link the dams (MMAyA, 2013). In addition to drinking water, the Misicuni Multipurpose Project is intended to serve as a source of hydroelectric energy, with the capacity to generate 120 MW, and a source of irrigation water. Thus, the project includes the construction of a hydroelectric centre in Molle Molle and irrigation infrastructure (MMAyA, 2013). The project guarantees a water supply guarantee of 2.486 L/s for irrigation and 5.038 L/s for drinking water (MMAyA, 2013).

Misicuni is an example of a high-modernist project typical of twentieth-century water management based on supply-side management principles. Initially, the Misicuni project was promoted as a regional development project for Cochabamba and viewed as compensation to the city for the rapid in-migration following the fall of the mining industry (Laurie & Marvin, 1999). Laurie and Marvin (1999, p. 1409) further argue that Misicuni formed part of the Cochabamba identity that is "strongly associated with a wider cultural and political project signalling the modernization of Cochabamba people and their region." Throughout the years, staunch support by local groups in Cochabamba ensured the Misicuni project's persistence (Hines, 2018). Whether or not it is still associated with the city's modernization, Misicuni survived waves of international swings in water management and today is propelled by central state support, claimed as a success of the MAS government.

The first feasibility fiscal studies conducted in the 1970s (1974, 1978–9) miscalculated the costs of Misicuni. Without a precedent for such a high-cost project in the country, Misicuni was deemed not viable. This was the beginning of a series of erroneous feasibility studies that served to delay the project further (Vera Varela, 1995). The project was again viewed as unaffordable during the economic and political crises in Bolivia from 1980–5, and international finance from the Inter-American Development Bank for another feasibility study was pulled in 1984 as national debt repayments were not met (Laurie & Marvin, 1999). In 1987, the state-owned Misicuni Company was formed, with an updated project estimate of USD 350 million. However, the government decided to invest instead in an international airport for the region (Vera Varela, 1995).

The lack of funding for Misicuni was tied to a shift away from big dam projects internationally (Laurie & Marvin, 1999), further complicated by the trend towards neoliberalism and privatization in the 1990s. President Gonzalo Sánchez de Lozada pushed back against Misicuni as unviable, as it did not fit with the political economic stance of an export-driven economy in service of debt repayment (Vera Varela, 1995). Funding for the Misicuni project was pulled in 1993, though certain construction financed by Italian cooperation went forward between 1992 and 1996 with the expectation of future privatization (Laurie & Marvin, 1999). However, Misicuni faced competition from another potential water project, Coraní Valles.

The hydroelectric plant in Coraní that had previously belonged to the national electric entity, ENDE, was privatized by a Bolivian and US consortium. While water was a by-product of energy generation, the private company (Coraní S.A., partly owned by Dominion Energy) held concession of the water sources from Palca River (Laurie & Marvin, 1999). Under the Law of Electricity, the company had exclusive rights over the reservoir to generate electricity, which also impacted farmers' ability to use the water for irrigation purposes (Bustamante, 2002). The company sought new venues for revenue and proposed an 11-km tunnel to transport water to Cochabamba under a "take or pay" contract, where the volume of water and price are fixed in contract and the buyer is bound to payment whether or not the volume of water is received (Nickson & Vargas, 2002). The USD 90 million project had an estimated construction period of one to two years (Nickson & Vargas, 2002). This cost was viewed by the World Bank as more feasible and thus preferred over the Misicuni project (SSB, 2000).

As mentioned previously, the Sánchez de Lozada government aligned with the World Bank, and faced pressure to cut subsidies to the Misicuni project in favour of Coraní (Assies, 2003). Yet if Semapa had signed a deal with Coraní at the time, it would have been difficult to finance and construct Misicuni in the future when it might be needed to fulfil water demands. The mayor of Cochabamba at the time pushed back, arguing that the Coraní project did not comply with procurement law (Nickson & Vargas, 2002). Local engineering and construction companies also supported this position, as Misicuni potentially provided them with better contract opportunities (Nickson & Vargas, 2002). People rejected the Coraní alternative because they had already invested financially and mentally into the "myth" of Misicuni and feared it would be otherwise forgotten (de la Fuente, Interview, 2014). De la Fuente confirms that Cochabambinos identified with Misicuni, as it signalled regional independence. Misicuni was favoured locally as a means of resisting the central state and establishing autonomy (Laurie & Marvin, 1999). Without a clear consensus between national and local authorities, institutions, and citizens on how to move forward, the Coraní project was eventually shelved (Vera Varela, 1995), yet reappears intermittently when Misicuni does not meet expectations.

The Coraní site is now back in the hands of the nationalized electric company, ENDE. The proposal to divert its water re-emerged during the 2016 drought crisis as an alternative to Misicuni. But it is now local powers—the Civic Committee (made up of Cochabamba professionals) and Semapa, both aligned with the Mayor's office—that support the Coraní project, whereas Misicuni is the project favoured by the federal government, MAS. Those in favour of Coraní argue that Misicuni is not the definitive solution. According to Semapa's General Manager at the time, Gamal Serhan, Misicuni is not the only source: "this was a mistake by those that conceived the Metropolitan Master Plan, and it is worthwhile that we immediately take up the issue of Coraní" ("Siete municipios se unen por una agenda de agua", 2016). As early as 2015, Mayor José Maria Leyes, was considering perforating wells to transport water from Coraní to mitigate water needs while waiting for Misicuni (Manzaneda, 2015). The Coraní project is supported by local powers that lean right politically, in opposition to the MAS government. Though there has been a reversal in which project municipal or state authorities favour, the fact remains that large hydrology projects are used strategically to match political agendas.

After the Coraní project was dismissed in the 1990s, Misicuni was reframed to suit neoliberal restructuring, as it was included as a water supplier to Semapa as part of the privatization contract with Aguas del Tunari (Laurie & Marvin, 1999). During the privatization period, the costs of completing Misicuni were transferred to water users through increased and unsustainable tariffs, forming one of the Water War movement's driving motivations (Assies, 2003).

Following the Water War, construction of the Misicuni project was underway once more, yet was perpetually delayed, paralyzed for months at a time, and shrouded in scandal and lack of transparency. It took eight years to finish the tunnel, four and a half years longer than projected. Now, with MAS as a proponent of the Misicuni project, the construction of the Misicuni Dam and related projects was slated to begin in 2007, but similarly experienced delays.

Contract irregularities were uncovered again in 2013, when accounts of fraud, fake consortiums, and opacity surrounding finances came to light. The Italian consortium *Grandi Lavori Ficosit* received a portion of a USD 78 million contract without a commitment to execute any work. This contract was rescinded, but the project lost money and construction was stalled. Finally, the Misicuni projects were reinitiated under a Supreme Decree (1946) in 2014 ("Ministerio aprueba $us 32 millones para Misicuni", 2014). The contract was eventually granted to Chinese corporation CAMCE, part of the growing influx of Chinese capital in Latin American development. Following some disputes over CAMCE's breach of labour laws, works were finally completed two years later, allowing Morales to claim the success for the project. He opened the valves of the dam for the first 450 L/s of water to be channelled to Cochabamba in 2017.

Misicuni Dam construction is now complete, and water is accumulating. However, there are ongoing issues: the amount of irrigation water is not at projected levels, and three adduction tunnels to bring water to municipalities are still under construction (Vásquez, 2021; Burgos, 2017). Concerns around Cochabamba's ageing water infrastructure's inability to receive the increased volume of water from Misicuni are confirmed through instances of overflow. Due to a burst pipe, 120,000 L of water drained into the streets, the equivalent of ten *aguatero* tanks. In the meantime, Cochabamba residents are still rationing water, especially in the Southern Zone. In mid-2021, the MMAyA signed a contract with Misicuni guaranteeing a 2 million boliviano (equivalent to USD 290,700) investment to construct a 15-km adduction to deliver water to this underserved zone. However, this requires Semapa to build corresponding infrastructure by April 2022. The Misicuni Dam, a project over 60 years in the making, purportedly has a lifecycle of under 20 years (G. Maldonado, Interview, 2014). Yet citizens of Cochabamba remain hesitantly optimistic for Misicuni to resolve their water problems: "People still have hope for Misicuni" (G. Zeballos, Interview, 2014). This perspective extends even to small-scale operators in the Southern Zone whose autonomy to self-govern their water systems may be adversely impacted by the arrival of Misicuni water (Marston, 2014).

Part of the uncertainty and incoherence surrounding Misicuni can be linked to poor implementation of public participation. Despite efforts to lift the obscurity surrounding Misicuni's finances and contracts by making certain information public, the scheme has retained its characteristics as a highly technical project, largely inaccessible to the average citizen. The veneration of "expert knowledge" continues in the MAS era despite the rhetoric of participation and social control. This is most evidenced by recent scandals, where citizens denounced the lack of transparency surrounding the project ("Misicuni formula nuevo cronograma", 2015). Importantly, there is no robust mechanism for citizen input on Misicuni.

The most vocal demands for social control and participation in the Misicuni project are made by irrigators, Indigenous and *campesino* communities surrounding the project sites seeking compensation for the detrimental effects of construction. Their livelihoods depend on the water resources which are being diverted by project construction. The response to their demands has largely been one akin to social corporate responsibility. Displaced communities affected by the destruction of their establishments (churches, cemeteries, etc.) are compensated in an ad hoc manner with improved housing and new community centres and schools, which are largely viewed as incommensurable by affected communities (Hoogendam & Boelens, 2019). The tensions surrounding territorial rights and access to resources for the inhabitants close to Misicuni are often overlooked in research and debates surrounding Misicuni, which most often focus on advancements or delays in completion. Regalsky (2015) highlights the ways in which urban water services have rural implications, how the fast pace of urbanization is changing land use and water demands and shifting power dynamics between the state and Indigenous and *campesino* groups, whose organizational strength has been affected by the co-optation of their leaders by the MAS regime. Zimmerer (2015) argues that MAS has adopted a river-basin approach to water governance mixed with "Indigenous state talk," which incorporates Indigenous concepts into rhetoric and policies that con-tradict actual water management practices of Indigenous and *campesino* groups. However, by assigning Indigenous values to water projects, MAS defends its position and differentiates the party's politics from modernist or neoliberal foundations of the projects even when the problems of non-transparency, fraud, corruption, and community displacement have been consistent across different governments.

This process of co-optation exemplifies MAS's efforts to control politi-cal space (Tockman & Cameron, 2014). Among MAS supporters, there is a noted shift from defending autonomy, or what is "ours," to relying on the state. Weakened opposition from even the most militant of these groups in Cochabamba, FEDECOR, is linked to MAS's interference (Zimmerer, 2015). Nevertheless, groups still do feel ownership over the *proceso de cambio* (process of change) initiated by MAS, and it is used as a protest slo-gan against MAS members when their actions are contested. Some groups of irrigators continue to oppose the Misicuni project, which they claim is in violation of their uses and customs related to water rights. These antago-nisms bring into focus questions of who has access to water, the power to enjoy water rights, and the power to influence these decisions.

Looking forward: The Metropolitan Master Plan for Water Services and the Water Agenda

The foregoing issues can be compared against two more recent water gov-ernance initiatives: the Metropolitan Master Plan for Water and the Water Agenda. These two documents, both developed via government collabo-ration reflect two different approaches to resolving Cochabamba's water problems. The Master Plan is a technical report with largely nominal par-ticipation, while the Water Agenda is a conceptual document that priori-tizes meaningful citizen engagement. Though the Water Agenda is not a response to the Metropolitan Master Plan nor conceived of as its alternative, it is useful to compare these two initiatives that present widely different approaches. Table 5.2 provides a brief overview of the main comparison points, while the following section examines how each fits into the partici-patory framework developed in this book.

Table 5.2 Comparison of the Metropolitan Master Plan and the Water Agenda

Metropolitan Master Plan	Water Agenda
• Technical report • Developed by external consultants • National government initiative • No explicit mention of participation and/or social control • Consultation with certain community water providers • Public presentation of results (report itself initially not widely disseminated) • Nominal participation	• Conceptual document • Developed by local water experts • Led by Cochabamba's Integrated Water Planning and Management Department • Public participation clearly stated as a priority • Conference and workshops for public input • Potential for transformative participation

The Metropolitization of Services: The Metropolitan Master Plan for Water Services

In 2012, the Ministry of Environment and Water contracted a group of consultants from four multinational companies—Técnica y Projectos (Spain), Gitec Consult (Germany), Land and Water Bolivia (Bolivia), and Aguilar and Asociados (Bolivia, Venezuela)—to conduct studies and elaborate plans for resolving water problems in the major Bolivian cities of La Paz-El Alto, Santa Cruz, and Cochabamba. The Spanish Cooperation (FECASALC) and the Inter-American Development Bank financed the multiple-city study (MMAyA, 2013). The resulting Metropolitan Master Plan (PMM) for water services in Cochabamba encompasses the city of Cochabamba and its six neighbouring municipalities, designed to "unify the levels of service, improve and share water services" (PMM Consultant, Interview, 2014). One Cochabamba engineer dubbed this the "metropolitization" of services: though the service providers might be municipalities or small-scale community providers, the quality of service would be uniform across the metropolitan area. However, there was no clear consensus as to how this ideal might be accomplished, and, given that the Master Plan had only minimal consultation with water users and community groups, its participation can be categorized as nominal at best.

At its heart, the Master Plan is conceived as a vehicle to deliver Misicuni water, requiring 1,000 L/s of drinking water and 1,000 L/s of irrigation water to be sold at price that recuperates costs, but is also affordable to all (PMM Consultant, Interview, 2014). For the entire Cochabamba metropolis, the plan estimates a staggering USD 555,600,000 over 20 years to complete eight potable water projects, seven sanitation and sewage projects, and improve infrastructure and service operations, including the existing Albar-rancho wastewater treatment plant in Cochabamba. Eleven chapters of the report offer technical analysis of the current water situation and detailed project proposals. As databases on water in Cochabamba are few, the consultant explained they had to "start from zero" (PMM Consultant, Interview, 2014). The main management proposal is that the different governing bodies, from the municipal service Semapa to the rural services at the edges of the metropolis, be coordinated under one integrated system and be overseen by one governing body, a public water utility to coordinate all services in the metropolitan area (Rodriguez, Interview, 2014). This metropolitization is therefore intended to unify levels of service, improve them, and share water with the aim of avoiding water conflicts and disputes.

To date, there is no plan to indicate an overarching governance structure or how it might operate. Many named Semapa as the most logical entity to undertake the responsibility for the metropolitan zone. The manager of Semapa's Transparency Unit affirmed that Semapa was best suited, as they were the largest municipal utility in the region, and others defended Semapa's suitability for this role, citing the company's experience. However, during the process of elaborating the Master Plan, Semapa was largely absent from discussions and did not contribute to the document (Rodriguez, Interview, 2014). Given Semapa's poor track record servicing the city of Cochabamba, it is unsurprising that some are sceptical of its ability to expand to this role: "it would be more of the same, strengthening the logic of over-consumption, squandering already scarce water" (Crespo, Interview, 2014). Despite cynicism towards Semapa, many agree that a metropolitan company is a practical solution, based on the fact that water flows through all municipalities in a single water catchment area, reflecting a river-basin approach (Ledo, Interview, 2014).

In the metropolitan area of Cochabamba, only three of seven municipalities are serviced by municipal water providers; the remainder depend on small-scale community operators. These small-scale operators are presented as an important part of the water equation in the Master Plan, and strategies for their institutional strengthening are central to its vision. This inclusion likely arose from civil society pressure to include small-scale operators and to consult local actors: "In Cochabamba, people fight, kill, for water. If they want to impose a governing model from above once more, it will be another disaster" (Caneda, Interview, 2014). Reference to small-scale water operators occurred only after an outcry over comments made by a government official that smaller operators will eventually make way for a metropolitan company to manage water. Though the statements were later recanted, it is a common perspective amongst many people I interviewed in the Bolivian water sector that water committees will or should eventually be absorbed into a municipal company such as Semapa. None of the interviewees elaborated on how Semapa might achieve this feat if they are currently unable to service the entire population of Cochabamba, let alone the entire metropolitan area. As of October 2021, the Misicuni Company was officially recognized as a certified potable water distributor, though no plans for centralizing the metropolitan region's water services through Misicuni were revealed. This repositioning places the future of small-scale operators into more uncertainty, even if they are cited as important in the Master Plan.

Disregard for small-scale water operators is evident throughout the region despite their official legal recognition, further complicated by fragmented and sometimes ill-considered international funding. The Master Plan design requires a coordinated effort, yet does not address the difficult task of developing and maintaining partnerships between municipalities that can have contentious relations. Organization and agreements are required to realize a metropolitan company (Paniagua, Interview, 2014).

A Bolivian NGO director called the document a "classic" master plan: sound engineering insofar as it outlines how Misicuni water could be delivered to each municipality, but failing to elaborate on how water will be distributed beyond that point (NGO Director, Interview, 2014). As a result, the Master Plan repeats the same mistake of privatization: insufficiently considering the role of water committees and cooperatives. Despite this, the designers behind the Master Plan defend their project as inclusive:

> Our proposal is to have a metropolitan company. The administration of potable water and sewage, and the treatment plants to be managed by one operator. That said, we are not saying that small operators will disappear—they will continue to exist within their neighbourhoods. We proposed building water storage tanks for Misicuni water, billed via macro-meter gauges. . . . The networks will remain [the communities'], the difference is [the inhabitants] will no longer use contaminated wells, but purchase good-quality water from a regulating entity. They will continue distributing using their own networks. The Master Plan does not reach the domestic networks; it reaches the distribution tanks.
> (PMM Consultant, Interview, 2014)

This idea of providing water to communities in bulk is a continuation of the current arrangement and agreement between Semapa and some communities. But this is not the reality for most committees who alternatively rely on wells or *aguateros*, and the confusion surrounding the debate on the future of small-scale providers is a source of tension amongst residents. With its focus on the overarching infrastructure, the plan does not address inequities between systems, the difficulty in financing and maintaining systems, and possible deficiencies such as contamination, leaks, and lack of sewage systems.

These oversights reflect the low level of public participation in the process of elaborating the Master Plan. According to one of the consultants on the project, participatory workshops were held in every municipality with the presence of local OTB representatives. However, not all of the small-scale water operators were consulted. In Cochabamba, collecting input from the organizations ASICA-SUDD-EPSAS and AGUAPAC was counted as public participation; however, they do not represent all water providers. Further, the organizers and consultants recognized these groups' presence and their legality as water providers, but they were only invited during the consultation phase, with a relatively low profile. The decision-making on the final outcomes of the Master Plan was a top-down process managed by the consultants, the MMAyA, and the departmental government. Some local actors I spoke with expressed disapproval or dissatisfaction with the process:

> The study that I saw was not very detailed, it was very superficial. The technicians came, added up how many [committees] existed. It was very superficial data. To undertake a study in Cochabamba, with all the diversity we have in water management, requires deep surveys, to serve as reasoning or focus on how the water could be managed.
>
> (Zeballos, Interview, 2014)

For the consultant working on the Master Plan, the process amounted to what he called an "inclusive participation," though he acknowledged hesitancy to show the costs of their plans for fear of alarming or dissuading the population (PMM Consultant, Interview, 2014). Upon completion, the Master Plan was not initially widely shared despite being a publicly funded document.

The Master Plan was approved in 2014 at the municipal, departmental, and federal levels. One engineer estimated that funding, design, and construction would require a minimum of four years, depending on the successful completion of Misicuni, which could further prolong projects (Rodriguez, Interview, 2014). In the city of Cochabamba, the Mayor announced that 19 projects received 70% financing from MMAyA (Manzaneda & Vargas, 2017). However, the expansion and upgrading of the Albarrancho wastewater treatment plant has been slow to begin, requiring USD 13 million (Vásquez, 2016). Other municipalities are similarly struggling to keep pace with infrastructure requirements: projects have stalled in Quillacollo, the municipalities of Vinto and Sipe Sipe do not yet have plans, and a tentative joint project for Tiquipaya and Colcapirhua was unsuccessful. These obstacles are unsurprising due to the complications of finding financing and a lack of coordinated effort putting the plan into action, which were not detailed within the Master Plan (Paniagua, Interview, 2014): "they are only papers, but there is no money or application" (Maldonado, Interview, 2014). Importantly, the Master Plan does not substantially tackle or address questions related to water distribution, service rates, coordination between municipalities, and the implications of the metropolitization of water services for small-scale operators. By framing the Master Plan as a technical report, the omission of these significant questions is excused, yet they remain crucial to water governance in Cochabamba.

The Water Agenda: A step towards transformative participation?

The Water Agenda (*Agenda del Agua*), developed by water experts in Cochabamba, emerged in 2012–3, at the same time as the Metropolitan Master Plan. In contrast to the Master Plan, the Water Agenda's goal is to provide a conceptual framework for water governance. It is not a technical report; rather, it presents a "new water management paradigm" based on Andean principles of equity, autonomy, and collective responsibility (Bellaubi & Bustamante, 2018, p. 5). The Water Agenda project originated at the Cochabamba Department Water Directorate or DGA (*Dirección de Gestión del Agua del Gobierno Autónomo de Cochabamba*). The institution is the first of its kind to coordinate amongst the disparate sectors and water users in the department of Cochabamba. A relatively new department created in 2013, its principal objective is to develop capacity to establish politics, plans, and instruments for water management in Cochabamba (Salazar, Interview, 2014). Prior to the DGA, there was no departmental service to oversee river-basin management that was not divided by sector; thus, the new institution reflects the management model made explicit in Bolivia's new Constitution.

The Water Agenda was conceived as an instrument of collaborative water governance. In comparison to the Master Plan, it is focused on social conceptions of water management rather than the elaboration of technical matters. It is based on experiences of water agendas elsewhere, particularly in Costa Rica and Mexico, which aim to democratize knowledge, improve institutional capacity, and broaden societal participation in water management (Segura Bonilla, 2002). The term agenda rather than plan or project signals that the document is not responding directly to water demand but is rather a conceptual and strategic commitment prior to elaborating a plan (in which a technical plan might be later embedded):

> It seemed like a way to explain to society, to institutions, before talking about projects to get water, and to provide water, we should be in agreement on what the water problem is, what aspects are under attack, or conflictive, because there is not water for everyone. We are altering the

quality of water, contaminating water, we are over-exploiting subterranean resources, we are neglecting water as a natural element. Many aspects are creating conflicts and disputes over water. So we said, we need to have a basis of a common understanding, of what the problem is. We need to have a base of principles in order to engage people and come to agreement on how we can change the situation. That is the first part of the agenda. When we have an agreement, a common manifesto, then we can go ahead with projects, actions, and initiatives.

In order to give answers to water issues, it's not just a technical matter. It's not even an economic matter, because in Bolivia there's more money [now], there's state cooperation to undertake projects. What's more important is the social and institutional issue of concepts and principles that cannot be solved by the technical, or with money. It needs to be solved with attitudes, shared visions, with agreements and engagement. And that's not easy, but it's what we are proposing with the agenda.

(Salazar, Interview, 2014)

Specifically, the water agenda is based around principles of equity, collective responsibility, and autonomy, meant to encourage reciprocity with water. The "Water Agenda manifesto" stipulates:

The elaboration of the Agenda, as a platform for collective action is a political process and should be a construction of a common world that we all share in equivalence, with the same rights and obligations. It . . . is in our hands to define the agreements necessary for institutional, communal actions and personal relations with water, and at the same time, concrete forms to local autonomy.

In the same vein, recognizing the rights of Mother Earth obliges the participation of everyone in the solution of the water predicament and not only the State and institutions, because for invoking her, there is no privileged spokesperson. We are all inalienably part of her as we are of her community, the community of Earth.

(AdA, 2014)

Heavy discourse on Indigenous concepts such as respect for Mother Earth is a reflection of what Zimmerer (2015, p. 322) terms the Bolivian government's practices of "speaking like an Indigenous state . . . linguistic usage, the impression of consensus among ethnicities, and a conceptual hollowing." As noted earlier, the MAS government has utilized rhetoric of sustainable resource management and the protection of Mother Earth while pursuing a resource-extractive model of economic growth. However, the DGA goes beyond discourse and symbolism in their attempt to establish a mechanism for local level community engagement and multi-scalar water governance. Within the Water Agenda itself, public participation is underlined as essential.

However, the DGA also supports a river-basin approach, emerging from the Dublin Principles of 1992, which has nevertheless garnered critique as the logical unit for water management and planning (Quiroz, 2012, p. 71). Specifically, some communal territories in Bolivia challenge the concept (Cossío & Wilk, 2017). In these spaces, water is managed traditionally though uses and customs, negotiated between communities in the context of communal territories and their local water systems, not at the river-basin level (Cossío & Wilk, 2017). According to Molle (2009, p. 492), "political or administrative boundaries seldom correspond to watershed lines, and the socio-economic forces and processes." The natural limits of resources do not necessarily correspond with administrative and political boundaries. For example, the scale of the water basin is not a main consideration to communities in their daily water management and practices: "the abstract conceptions of space such as found in definitions of river basins or water systems are mediated by science while conceptions of space by local populations are based on empirical knowledge" (Cossío & Wilk, 2017, p. 192). For Cossío and Wilk (2017), the approach may be inadequate because it imposes a notion of abstract space onto communities that use and share water in concrete and dynamic ways. The practices that have met water needs of marginalized communities have largely occurred on a smaller scale. The introduction of the river-basin framework has pushed communities to adopt the perspective and terminology to access technical assistance and negotiate water conflicts within this particular model (Cossío & Wilk, 2017; Bellaubi & Bustamante, 2018). This exemplifies Zimmerer's (2015) point of the contradictions of the "Indigenous state" upholding "Indigenous values" rhetorically but encouraging a "not-quite-neoliberal" water management strategy in practice.

Cochabamba's DGA is partially a reflection of national policy that combines Indigenous discourse and neoliberal concepts. However, the perspective of the DGA, as interpreted through the Water Agenda, appears to be a departure from mainstream conceptualization of integrated water management, as it leaves out discussions of water pricing but includes the concept of *usos y costumbres* and participation to democratize decision-making. The director of the department called upon people's participatory spirit exemplified during the Water War to extend to water planning and management. In practice, the meetings where the agenda was penned were directed and attended by water experts in the Cochabamba water sector, searching for solutions to the water problems in the region. Though water experts put together the agenda, the department has actively engaged the public in their events. The Water Agenda was presented to social organizations, academics, and politicians for discussion, most notably in a series of water conferences. Representatives from seven municipalities and 150 participants attended a water conference in 2016 to primarily deal with the drought situation but also to advance the Water Agenda by generating policies. Topics of discussion included access to water resources, economy of water, the potential of establishing a conflict resolution body, and how river-basin management can build a new norm around the relationship to water—how to recycle water, gather rainwater, and contaminate less. In this sense, the Water Agenda goes beyond the Metropolitan Master Plan in its inclusive attempt to address governance matters. By featuring different practices and perspectives around water and implementing public participation within water management, the Water Agenda provides a mechanism towards more transformative participation.

Conclusion

The Metropolitan Master Plan and the Water Agenda present distinct approaches and understandings to water management in Cochabamba. The documents are a physical proof of the competing perspectives of participation in water management. The government support for both initiatives illustrates how the state does not necessarily operate with coherence (Gupta, 1995). The nationally-commissioned Master Plan was approved by local authorities and hinges on the heavily invested Misicuni Multipurpose Project that forms part of the regional collective imagination. The Water Agenda, a more collaborative effort, nevertheless is tied to a departmental-level governing body, championed by actors within the institution. Whereas the technical Master Plan misses the fundamental issue of *how* water distribution will be coordinated, the Water Agenda accurately depicts the local realties and reflects the tensions of water management in Cochabamba as it proposes a participatory process to rethink the relationship with water. Bellaubi and Bustamante (2018, p. 12) understand the Water Agenda as an "ongoing politically contested political process" that opens a path to overcome territorial conflicts resulting from contradictory MAS water policies by way of negotiated agreements and consultation with local knowledge and practices to "build a common sustainable vision of water." The Water Agenda has not yet achieved wide acceptance from all actors in the Cochabamba Valley; trepidation towards the plan on behalf of some political authorities and fragmented civil society actors present barriers to the process proposed in the Water Agenda (Bellaubi & Bustamante, 2018). For the more progressive vision of water management in the Water Agenda to prevail, greater coordination between institutions and actors is required.

References

Agenda del Agua (AdA). (2016). *Estrategia ADA 2016–2020, 2016.* Agenda del Agua.

Assies, W. (2003). David versus Goliath in Cochabamba. *Latin American Perspectives, 30*(3), 14–36. https://doi.org/10.1177/0094582X03030003003

Bellaubi, F., & Bustamante, R. (2018). Towards a new paradigm in water management: Cochabamba's water agenda from an ethical approach. *Geosciences, 8*(177). https://doi.org/doi:10.3390/geosciences8050177

Burgos, C. (2017). Cochabamba continuá sin recibir agua de Misicuni. *Los Tiempos.* https://m.lostiempos.com/actualidad/local/20170907/cochabamba-continua-recibir-agua-misicuni

Bustamante, R. (2002). *Legislación del agua en Bolivia.* UMSS Centro AGUA.

Cossío, V., & Wilk, J. (2017). A paradigm confronting reality: The river basin approach and local water management spaces in the Pucara Basin, Bolivia, *Water Alternatives 10*(1), 14.

Gupta, A. (1995). Blurred boundaries: The discourse of corruption, the culture of politics, and the imagined state. *American Ethnologist, 22*(2), 375–402. JSTOR.

Hines, S. (2018). The power and ethics of vernacular modernism: The Misicuni dam project in Cochabamba, Bolivia, 1944–2017. *Hispanic American Historical Review, 98*(2), 223–256. https://doi.org/10.1215/00182168-4376680

Hoogendam, P., & Boelens, R. (2019). Dams and damages: Conflicting epistemological frameworks and interests concerning "compensation" for the Misicuni project's socio-environmental impacts in Cochabamba, Bolivia. *Water, 11*(3), 408. https://doi.org/10.3390/w11030408

Laurie, N., & Marvin, S. (1999). Globalisation, neoliberalism, and negotiated development in the Andes: Water projects and regional identity in Cochabamba, Bolivia. *Environment and Planning A, 31*(8), 1401–1415.

Ministerio aprueba $us 32 millones para Misicuni, Cochabamba. (2014). *Los Tiempos.* https://www.lostiempos.com/actualidad/local/20140402/ministerio-aprueba-us-32-millones-misicuni.

Misicuni formula nuevo cronograma, Cochabamba. (2015). *Los Tiempos.* https://www.lostiempos.com/actualidad/local/20150626/misicuni-formula-nuevo-cronograma

Manzaneda, L. (2015, October 23). La pampa, mercado que menos agua recibe. *Los Tiempos.*

Manzaneda, L., & Vargas, J. (2017). Pugna entre Semapa y Misicuni se intensifica. *Los Tiempos.* https://www.lostiempos.com/actualidad/local/20170411/pugna-semapa-misicuni-se-intensifica

Marston, A. J. (2014). The scale of informality: Community-run water systems in peri-urban Cochabamba, Bolivia. *Water Alternatives, 7*(1), 72–88.

MMAyA. (2013). *Plan Maestro Metropolitano de Agua y Saneamiento del Area Metropolitano de Cochabmba.* Ministerio del Agua, Viceministerio de Riego.

Molle, F. (2009). River-basin planning and management: The social life of a concept. *Geoforum, 40*(3), 484–494. https://doi.org/10.1016/j.geoforum.2009.03.004

Nickson, A., & Vargas, C. (2002). The limitations of water regulation: The failure of the Cochabamba Concession in Bolivia. *Bulletin of Latin American Research, 21*(1), 99–120.

Quiroz, F. (2012). La gestión integral e los recursos hídricos. Paradigma con desafíos y oportunidades. In F. Quiroz, O. Delgadillo, & A. Durán (Eds.), *Aguas arriba, aguas abajo. Luces y sombras de la Gestión Integral de los Recursos Hídricos: Reflexiones desde la investigación aplicada* (pp. 29–79). Plural editores.

Regalsky, P. (2015). *El Proyecto Misicuni y la territorialidad originaria (TCO) de Ayopaya* (Territorios, minifundio, e individualización). Tierra.

Segura Bonilla, O. (2002). Agenda ambiental del agua en Costa Rica. *Revista Geográphica de América Central*, *1*(40), 39–49.

Siete municipios se unen por una agenda de agua, Cochabamba. (2016). *Los Tiempos*. https://www.lostiempos.com/actualidad/local/20160623/siete-municipios-se-unen-agenda-del-agua

Superintendencia de Saneamiento Básico (SSB), (2000). Informe sobre el contrato de concesión para el aprovechamiento de agua y los servicios de agua potable y alcantarillado sanitario de la ciudad de Cochabamba, Bolivia. *Superintendencia de Saneamiento Básico*.

Tapia Callao, W. (2020). Misicuni concluye obras, pero agua no llegará al sur. *Los Tiempos*. https://www.lostiempos.com/actualidad/cochabamba/20200923/misicuni-concluye-obras-pero-agua-no-llegara-al-sur

Tockman, J., & Cameron, J. (2014). Indigenous autonomy and the contradictions of plurinationalism in Bolivia. *Latin American Politics and Society*, *56*(3), 46–69. https://doi.org/10.1111/j.1548-2456.2014.00239.x

Vásquez, K. (2016). Sacaba, pionera en reusar aguas negras. *Los Tiempos*. https://www.lostiempos.com/actualidad/local/20160927/sacaba-pionera-reusar-aguas-negras

Vásquez, K. (2021). Misicuni está a "un paso" de acabar dos ductos para cuatro municipios. *Los Tiempos*. https://www.lostiempos.com/actualidad/cochabamba/20211017/misicuni-esta-paso-acabar-dos-ductos-cuatro-municipios

Vera Varela, R. (1995). *Misicuni: La frustración de un pueblo?* Aliaga.

Zimmerer, K. S. (2015). Environmental governance through "speaking like and Indigenous state" and respatializing resources: Ethical livelihood concepts in Bolivia as versatility or versimilitude? *Geoforum*, *64*, 314–324.

6 Conclusion
Building a common path

The reversal of water privatization in Cochabamba is considered a victory of collective action. Following the Water War of 2000, the people of Cochabamba were highly motivated to (re)build a public alternative to improve water services for all residents. Today, the unfortunate reality is a water utility unable to deliver on that ideal. While piecemeal improvements can be noted, two decades since the Water War, access to water and sanitation remains uneven and chaotic amid cycles of severe water shortages. The municipal water utility Semapa reverted to the pre-privatization status quo of a state-led, unwieldy company that does not deliver on expectations of social control in public water management. As a result, many Cochabambinos associate the remunicipalization process with regression to an inadequate and opaque government administration.

This study of remunicipalization in Cochabamba hopes to contribute to this debate. Understanding disappointment is just as important to strengthening public alternatives as understanding success, helping to identify impediments and pathways towards the building of a more effective public water provider in the future. Despite the scandals surrounding Semapa and Misicuni over the years, the case of Cochabamba has not been a conspiracy towards the failure of public water management. Rather, a confluence of factors—including power struggles, mismatched ideologies, lack of resources, difficult topography, chaotic and wanting urban planning—has meant there is no straightforward answer on how to move forward and resolve the city's water issues. As demonstrated in the preceding chapters, the answer to the question of democratic public control of water services in Cochabamba lies in part in competing interpretations and implementations of public participation that contributed to the difficulty of rebuilding a strong public water utility. The central contribution of this book has been to unpack these different conceptualizations and mechanisms of participation and identify the nuances of participation in practice.

DOI: 10.4324/9781003169383-6

Applying this kind of typological framework has its limits, of course, as it sets up ideal types and practices of participation that do not always fit exactly into the established categories. Nevertheless, there are defining elements of practice that generally can be identified or tied to each classification. The exercise of applying the framework to the Bolivian context illustrates that all three (reformative, transformative, and nominal) types of participation can be found to varying degrees throughout the county's history, with the tools and practices of participatory mechanisms not necessarily matching their initial intent. The framework helps to illustrate how, in their implementation, participatory practices can be distorted or appropriated to serve different ends. Noting how policies and actions can shift from one category of participation to another also demonstrates how participation is not linear in practice. As such, using this participation typology as a conceptual framework challenges an unchecked celebration of notions of participation.

Throughout the book, I have contended that the ways people comprehend participation and actually participate in it is key to understanding the mixed results of Cochabamba's remunicipalization process. Disagreements between Semapa's administration, the municipal government, technical experts, Semapa's union, and the water movement, including clashes among progressive forces, prevented a consensus. In this manner I was able to argue that the outcome in Semapa has been a nominal form of participation, mirroring the broader context in MAS's Bolivia where the government's rhetoric of change and policies of social control and participation have largely been nominal and have not resulted in transformative change.

Enhanced *co-gestion:* A proposal for change

Moving forward, how can Cochabambinos build an "ideal" public water system with quality, continuous services at a fair price which "ensures everyone has access to water" (de la Fuente, Interview, 2014)? A key component of this ideal is repoliticizing public participation (Hickey & Mohan, 2005) and redistributing power to allow people to exercise their agency in decision-making spaces. The peri-urban zones that suffer the most water injustice need be prioritized, and public participation is key to understanding the particular needs of these neighbourhoods. As a first step towards a more transformative model of participation, I suggest enhancing the existing model of water *co-gestion* or co-management in Cochabamba to strengthen the labour–community alliance. In the following, I outline the proposal's potential benefits and explore the conditions and challenges to its implementation, namely, worker and neighbourhood engagement, ecological considerations, political support, and public financing.

Labour–community coalition

A starting point for improving public participation is through building alliances between the peri-urban communities and Semapa workers. The relationship between Semapa workers and residents of Cochabamba has been fraught since the period following the Water War, when Semapa's union actively undermined efforts of increasing institutional social control to maintain their relative position of power (Wainwright, 2012; Spronk et al., 2012). Therefore, repairing this relationship and rebuilding lost trust is crucial to reforming a sense of solidarity between workers and communities that could lead to more active participation within Semapa.

The proposal put forth here is to strengthen this relationship by building upon the existing model of *co-gestion*, or co-management. In short, *co-gestion* typically consists of an agreement between Semapa and small-scale community water systems to purchase water from Semapa in bulk, while maintaining separate and autonomous water systems and governance structures. *Co-gestion* sometimes involves Semapa supporting these systems and sharing technology and techniques to help sustain the systems in an ad hoc fashion (O. Olivera, Interview, 2014). There was a short-lived worker-volunteer program where Semapa workers offered assistance to the technical maintenance of these systems, but this program was eventually dissolved due to lack of support. Ramping up these efforts in a more deliberate and sustained way could lead to more trust, communication, and collaboration and result in positive changes for the city's water sector.

For Semapa, accepting and implementing participatory mechanisms to incorporate citizen input into planning can prevent costly construction delays and conflicts. Assigning dedicated workers to each neighbourhood could help address one of the biggest challenges in Cochabamba's water governance, that is, of understanding the specific needs of each neighbourhood. In turn, Semapa workers can learn about participation and transparency from communitarian systems through their processes of communal decision-making, a model of governance that ensures social control by users who are acquainted with the needs of the community (APAAS President, Interview, 2014). Small-scale systems illustrate the potential of transformative participation, yet urbanization is changing the landscape, and with urban dwellers expanding into peripheral spaces on the urban–rural fringe, some of the culture and traditions of active participation are lost (Luisaga Puntiti, Interview, 2014). This worker–community alliance could help preserve models of transformative participation and inspire creative ways of implementing public participation within Semapa.

Mutual understanding already exists to some degree, as many of the Semapa workers' own water services are provided by their neighbourhood water committees and cooperatives. However, a challenge will be to set aside long-simmering tensions between these groups, not to mention the tensions that can exist within and amongst neighbourhoods. The strength of collective action has declined since Morales took office and the "state arrived" (Crespo, Interview, 2014). Additionally, the Right to Water narrative in Bolivia has shifted the lens through which people engage with water, creating a more confrontational situation that pits communities and different interest groups against each other, resulting in a more fragmented water movement. The initiative proposed here would require each neighbourhood to be paired with a set of workers to provide equal attention to each zone. The initiative could also face opposition from the union, as it would create additional demands on the workers. Therefore, Semapa would need to establish appropriate recognition and compensation for those involved.

Enabling ecological public services

Enhanced *co-gestion* would also require a change in thinking in terms of ecological concerns. Given the ecological limits to water in the region, there needs to be a smarter, more efficient use of water that limits overconsumption and redistributes water equally across the city (for example, by higher consumption being charged a higher rate). Improvement of the water recycling process and preserving green spaces in the city could also serve to combat deforestation (Gandarillas, Interview, 2014). An emphasis on water treatment and reuse towards other functions through different technologies requires education and a shift in attitudes (Bustamante, Interview, 2014). For example, communities have previously objected to the construction of wastewater treatment plants in their neighbourhoods. Here, *co-gestion* would have to move beyond the water delivery transaction, which has been its primary focus thus far, and towards a consideration of water at every point of the hydrosocial cycle in order to emphasize the common benefits of wastewater facilities. The *Agenda del Agua* could provide a conceptual starting point for a more comprehensive approach to water governance. These shifts would also require investment in infrastructure which has been lacking in the region, which leads into the next condition: political will and public funding.

Political support and public funding

Strengthening the labour–community component of the current model of *co-gestion* in Semapa requires dedicated resources and political support from the municipality, which arguably present the largest hurdles of the past two decades. The high turnover in Semapa's administration adds another layer of difficulty in prioritizing a program or initiative. Many people in Semapa, as well as technical water experts and government officials, equate "public" with "state" in terms of municipal services. Given the increased enthusiasm for the metropolitization of services in Cochabamba that favours larger governing bodies as the long-term solution for regional water governance, there may not be support for an initiative that further bolsters community-run systems.

Currently, the local authorities tend to latch onto the notion of "water scarcity" to excuse their inaction, even though a reorganization of the water delivery systems could provide the necessary water to each person or household. Stricter regulations for clandestine connections could help create a fairer system, though here again officials tend to avoid regulatory measures for fear of provoking another Water War (Paniagua, Interview, 2014). Further, in regional and local elections, officials do not want to install or improve water infrastructure because it disrupts or disturbs people; they prefer to support superficial, highly visible projects to ensure votes (Dávila-Poblete, Interview, 2016). Often, no clear proposals for water are made during elections (Oropesa, Interview, 2014). This inaction suggests there would be little impetus politically to support a coalition-building project that has no apparent tangible benefits.

Finally, in a not-so-post-neoliberal context, the market economy poses constraints to all public water providers, as the relatively de-commodified public water company remains embedded in a global marketplace. Meanwhile, the bottled water industry in Cochabamba continues to operate despite the sale of such water being illegal according to the Constitution. Extracting water for sale while the city does not have enough funds to satisfy demands by residents for public water is a practice that needs to be addressed. Policies should be implemented to better regulate the *aguateros* sector without disrupting the livelihood of these workers, who are themselves struggling to make a living. As the funding model for water and sanitation remains unchanged—largely financed by international donors—water management remains subject to global trends and constraints. Many community-run water systems have heretofore been supported through outside assistance, albeit applied inconsistently, which has resulted in shifting the responsibility of providing services away from local authorities. Now that this trend is on the wane, public funding is all the more crucial to ensure access to potable water for all. It remains to be seen whether the newly elected leaders of "MAS 2.0," President Luis Arce Catacora and Vice President David Choquehuanca will recommit to a sustainable water and sanitation sector and reconcile with the country's grassroots movements (Bjork-James, 2021).

Nearly twenty years following the Water War, the divisiveness among Cochabambinos impedes participation and thereby hinders resolving the water problem, which necessitates a coordinated effort. As historian Rafael Fuente puts it, Bolivians are tremendous in times of war and disastrous in times of peace.[1] Once the threat of privatization passed, the organizational capacity that manifested during the Water War also subsided. The power of collective action needs to be harnessed once more to address the difficult task of building an effective and equitable water system. An enhanced version of co-management that emphasizes understanding and coalition-building presents a first step towards forging a common path.

Conclusion

This book attempts to provide conceptual clarity on notions of participation by creating a typology of reformative, transformative, and nominal participation without negating local contexts. Adopting this lens of participation to analyze other instances of remunicipalization around the world could be a useful exercise to build a comparative guide. In turn, documenting cases where public participation has been more successfully integrated into models of water delivery or other types of public services (Fiasconaro, 2020) could provide useful strategies for Cochabamba. The participation framework developed here can be extended to the analysis of other public services as well, contributing to an understanding of the motivating factors behind social movements and how they strengthen or unravel. The lens of participatory water governance can also help understand the rural–urban tensions that arise with shifting land use in Cochabamba's peri-urban zone and how rapid infrastructural changes over the past three decades have shifted the landscape and reconfigured social dynamics.

In the context of fast-paced urbanization, uneven burdens of climate change, and the Covid-19 crisis, the importance of democratizing water and achieving universal access to public services is imperative (McDonald et al., 2020; Stoler et al., 2020; Sultana, 2021). There is much to be learned from further inquiry into water politics, which provide a window into the broad range of socio-economic dynamics within contemporary Bolivia and beyond. Understanding the roles that various actors play in participatory water governance can shed light on the political processes of water systems to uncover the shared aims of water governance.

Note

1 Presentation, PMM, Universidad Católica, Cochabamba, 26 February 2014.

References

Bjork-James, C. (2021). We are MAS 2.0. *NACLA Report on the Americas*, *53*(1), 7–11.

Fiasconaro, M. (2020). Knowledge-creation and sharing through public-public partnership in the water sector. In S. Kishimoto, L. Steinfort, & O. Petitjean (Eds.), *The future is public*. Transnational Institute.

Hickey, S., & Mohan, G. (2005). Relocating participation within a radical politics of development. *Development and Change*, *36*(2), 237–262. https://doi.org/10.1111/j.0012-155X.2005.00410.x

McDonald, D. A., Spronk, S., & Chavez, D. (2020). *Public water and COVID-19: Dark clouds and silver linings*. Municipal Services Project; Transnational Institute; CLASCO.

Spronk, S., Crespo, C., & Olivera, M. (2012). Struggles for water justice in Latin America. In D. A. McDonald & G. Ruiters (Eds.), *Alternatives to privatization: Public options for essential services in the Global South*. HSRC Press.

Stoler, J., Jepsen, W. E., & Wutich, A. (2020). Beyond handwashing: Water insecurity undermines COVID-19 response in developing areas. *Journal of Global Health*, *10*(1), 010355.

Sultana, F. (2021). Critical climate justice. *The Geographical Journal*, 1–7. https://doi.org/10.1111/geoj.12417

Wainwright, H. (2012). Transformative resistance: The role of labour and trade unions in alternatives to privatization. In D. A. McDonald & G. Ruiters (Eds.), *Alternatives to privatization: Public options for essential services in the Global South*. HSRC Press.

Index

Note: Numbers in *italics* indicate figures and numbers in **bold** indicate tables on the corresponding page.

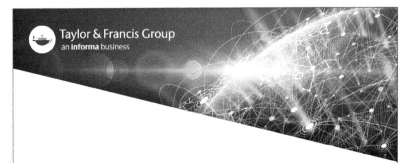

www.ingramcontent.com/pod-product-compliance
Ingram Content Group UK Ltd.
Pitfield, Milton Keynes, MK11 3LW, UK
UKHW020417010325
455677UK00029B/926